New Nations and Peoples

Egypt

Egypt

GORDON WATERFIELD

with 71 illustrations and 2 maps

New York
WALKER AND COMPANY

© Thames and Hudson 1967

All rights reserved. No portion of this work may be reproduced without permission except for brief passages for the purpose of review

Library of Congress Catalog Card Number: 67-13244

First published in the United States of America in 1967 by Walker and Company, a division of Publications Development Corporation

Printed in Great Britain by Jarrold and Sons Ltd, Norwich

Contents

Introduction

'Egypt is a palimpsest, in which the Bible is written over Herodotus and the Koran over that.'   Lady Duff Gordon

WORKING HALF-NAKED in the fields the Fellaheen look very like the figures on the walls of the ancient monuments; some are still using similar farm implements and boats on the Nile which has controlled the rhythm of their lives generation after generation for many thousands of years. From the beginning of history, government in Egypt has been centralized as much as possible in order to ensure the defence of a flat country and to make the best use of the river for agriculture, since there is little rainfall and most of the country is desert; out of a total of 386,198 square miles, only 13,500 are settled and cultivated. For over eight hundred miles the Nile flows from the southern Egyptian frontier near Wadi Halfa between the Libyan Desert on the west and the Arabian Desert on the east to the apex of the Delta twelve miles south of Cairo; between the bare granite and limestone ranges of Upper Egypt the river is so restricted that for most of the distance it only fertilizes a narrow strip of land, and the average rainfall is less than one inch.

The cultivated area is like a fan with a very long handle; from the apex near Cairo there is a triangle of very fertile land, laced with canals, with its base on the Mediterranean coast, where the rainfall averages eight inches a year. In ancient times the Nile had seven branches, but now there are only the Rosetta and Damietta branches which are about one hundred and fifty miles long, measuring from the apex of the Delta. Egypt, as Herodotus wrote, is indeed the gift of Nile.

Do the ancient Egyptians, so well described by Herodotus, have any connexion with modern Egyptians, or is Egypt, as stated in its Constitution, an Arab country? The well-known playwright, Tawfik al-Hakim, makes one of his characters in a novel say, 'can you really believe that the thousands of years which make up Egypt's past have vanished without a trace?' He is reported to be one of the favourite authors of President Gamal Abdel Nasser, and it has been stated that 'this idea that the descendants of the men who built the pyramids will once again astonish the world is fundamental to Nasser's thinking'.[1] President Nasser has referred to the many factors in Egypt's long history which are 'latent in our people's souls', and has stated that the period of the Pharaohs could not be over-looked, nor the interaction with Greek culture, nor the Roman invasion, nor, of course, the Arab Conquest and the waves of Arab immigration which followed.

For two thousand five hundred years, from the time of the invasion of the Persian conqueror Cambyses in 525 BC, foreigners ruled Egypt, except for a short period known as the Restoration in Pharaonic times; that memory has especially influenced Egyptian nationalists today: 'a study of Egyptian history will explain, even if it does not justify, everything that Nasser has said or done'.[2] Nasser is concerned, too, about what happened in the Middle Ages: 'if the Crusades marked the first dawnings of the Renaissance in Europe, they heralded the beginning of the ages of darkness in our country'.[3]

The picture of Egypt which has been given to Europe is a gloomy one because the travellers wrote of the Egyptians during periods of oppression, 'the ages of darkness'. Herodotus was there under the Persian occupation soon after the Egyptians had tried to revolt; others wrote when the country was under the occupation of Rome or Constantinople. European travellers from Britain, France, and Denmark began to visit Egypt in the seventeenth and eighteenth centuries when the people were impoverished by the oppressive rule of the later Circassian Mamelukes. Some account of these travellers is given here for their experiences reveal something of Egypt and of their own prejudices. 'Among the various commodities which are carried abroad by an Englishman when he first starts on his travels

8

in foreign lands', wrote Robert Curzon in the middle of the last century, 'is a good store, or outfit, of prejudices, prepossessions and convictions, which are founded on the nature of his education and have no vulgar reference to facts.'

Among these 'commodities' the most striking is the prejudice with regard to the religion of Islam. There has been a continuation of the battle fought out during the two hundred years of the Crusades between Christian and Muslim, ineffectively and uncomprehend/ ingly – the 'Great Debate' as Edward Gibbon called it. Many of the travellers and officials who came to Egypt believed that the religion of Islam was responsible for the backwardness of the people. William Kinglake prophesied in *Eothen* (1844) that Islam would wither away and the English, because of India, would plant a firm foot on the banks of the Nile and sit in the seats of the Faithful; that is what Cromer and his officials did forty years later. Cromer in his turn wrote that Islam was petrified, 'politically and socially moribund'. There are many eminent scholars to give the other side of the Debate. 'Islam is a living and vital religion', wrote Professor H. A. R. Gibb, 'appealing to the hearts, minds and conscience of tens and hundreds of millions, setting them a standard by which to live honest, sober and god/fearing lives. It is not Islam that is petrified, but its orthodox formulations. . . .' We find Lady Duff Gordon writing in the 1860s in her *Letters from Egypt* that she had been 'really amazed at several instances of English fanaticism. Why do people come to a Muslim country with such bitter hatred "in their stomachs". . . . There is a very general idea among Arabs that Christians hate the Muslims. They attribute to us the old crusading spirit.'

Some of the travellers are worth recalling, too, for their vivid descriptions. They were nearly all, often for different reasons, fas/ cinated by Egypt – even though most of them ignored the inhabitants. There are the colourful accounts of the Sphinx given by Kinglake and by Vivant Denon the painter, who gave us, too, a new insight into the beauty of the Pyramids: 'I should have liked to show them in that refined and transparent colouring they owe to the immense volume of air surrounding them'; Gustave Flaubert wrote about dawn seen from the top of the Great Pyramid of Giza, the mist dissolving over the Nile and the fertile fields below; Karnak seemed to him 'like the habitation of giants, where they must have served on gold plate whole men on skewers, like larks'. There are fine descriptions of Cairo looking down from Saladin's Citadel, and Gerard de Nerval has a picturesque account of the slave market in Cairo where he bought Zeynab. The travellers were amazed, as was Herodotus, by the country's many wonders; Burckhardt came upon the buried colossi of Abu Simbel with hardly anything showing except their 'bonnets', and Belzoni described digging them out and discovering the temple within. Egypt influenced Shakespeare, Byron, and Shelley, and the novels and plays of the French Romantics of the last century, while Alexandria inspired the fine Greek poet, Cavafy, of the twentieth century, and Lawrence Durrell's 'Alexandria Quartet'.

Then there were the strange ones; Eliza Fay in Alexandria, so delightfully described by E. M. Forster in his guide-book, and the Irish lady who climbed Pompey's Pillar and wrote a letter to the British Consul from the top. Englishmen fired off revolvers in the Great Pyramid of Giza and the serious Richard Lepsius planted a Christmas tree in the sarcophagus; among the strangest of the visitors perhaps was the Saint-Simonian, Prosper Enfantin, who came to Egypt at the time of Mohammed Ali to build a 'Suez Canal' and in quest of a woman who was 'predestined' to enable him to give birth to a new Messiah. They have all helped to enliven the more serious political story of the Egyptians.

'Fate has decreed', wrote President Nasser, 'that we should stand at the world's cross-roads; we have often been the invaders' passage-way and the target of adventurers.' In this book an attempt is made to look, to some extent, through Egyptian eyes at developments, such as the impact of Bonaparte's invasion which opened the way to a modern Egypt, and the subsequent British occupation which lasted in one form or another for over seventy years. A new conflict arose and imprecations against imperialism took the place of curses against the Christian infidel. The alien ideas and institutions from Europe destroyed the sociological patterns and 'brought a period of formlessness and irresponsibility deeply damaging to Middle Eastern policy and society. . . . The mood of admiration and imitation has given way to one of envious rancour. This change has no doubt been helped by our own lamentable political and moral failures; it has also been helped by the lessons of liberty and human self-respect which we of the West have taught.'[4]

Egypt's past history and the violent impact of Europe helps to explain aspects of present Egyptian policy, which are disapproved of by many in the West, and which remain difficult, often impossible, to understand if looked at from an entirely European or American viewpoint. The accounts of their policies given by the British and French up to the first quarter of the twentieth century are little concerned with what the Egyptians thought or their reactions to the West. It is, in fact, only in the last few decades that such detailed studies have been made in the writings of the late Louis Massignon, H. A. R. Gibb, Albert Hourani, Bernard Lewis, Jacques Berque, and others. It is only comparatively recently, too, that the West has been able to read books written by Egyptians and Arabs in which they have analysed their own problems. Gradually a new understanding is growing, but it has taken a remarkably long time. The disastrous Suez incident of the autumn of 1956 high-lighted British and French ignorance of the Middle East. It achieved something towards education, expensive though it was. Belatedly it forced Western statesmen to study Middle Eastern problems anew, to realize the extent of the resentment against the West, and to study the two revolutions taking place in the Arab world today. 'Side by side with the violent revolution against colonialism', states an Arab historian, 'there is going on within the Arab world a more silent but no less meaningful revolution against the ills and the diseases in the national body. There are internal battles as well as external battles: the battle against feudalism and economic injustice; the battle against ignorance, poverty and prejudice – the old battles for human dignity and human equality.'[5]

G.W.

1 Herodotus and the ancient Egyptians

'There is no country which possesses so many wonders'

THE LITTLE PICTURES AND SIGNS carved or painted on the walls of Egyptian temples and tombs, which came to be known as hieroglyphs, remained a mystery for many centuries. The fact that no one understood them added to the reputation for great wisdom possessed by the Egyptians, referred to several times in the Old Testament. It was known that they were a civilized, industrious, and artistic people from the many paintings and bas-reliefs on their monuments throughout the Nile Valley. These told with grace and vividness how they carried on agriculture, travelled in boats on the Nile, held festivals, married, fought battles, set up their monuments, worshipped strange gods with the heads of animals, respected the Pharaohs, how they died, were bewailed, mummified, and how their spirit was helped in its journey in the Other World.

The pictures told such a lively story and the monuments were so impressive that visitors to Egypt were filled with wonder; even the ancient Greeks, who prided themselves on their own wisdom and fine monuments, admitted, rather reluctantly, that Greece had learned much from Egypt. It was not before the sixth and fifth centuries BC, as far as we know, that the Greeks wrote any detailed account of Egypt; among those that survived, the most entertaining and informative is that written by Herodotus.

Egypt had been part of the Persian Empire for seventy-five years when Herodotus went there as a tourist in about 450 BC; he stayed for three and a half months from August to November, travelling in the Delta by boat during the flood time and up the

Nile as far as the First Cataract at Aswan. 'There is no country', he wrote, 'which possesses so many wonders, nor any that has such a number of works which defy description.' His account of Egypt makes up Book II of the nine books of his history, which describes the epic struggle between the Greeks and Persians. Others had written about Egypt, such as Hecataeus of Milo, but most of his account is lost, and there were later Greek writers, such as Diodorus Siculus and Strabo; but Herodotus' account remained the most popular and was still being used and discussed by eighteenth‑ and nineteenth‑century scholars and travellers. 'His vivid perception and simple, yet most graphic descriptions might have been written yesterday for the Past of Egypt is its Present.'[6] Several of the expres‑ sions used by Herodotus and other Greek writers remain to this day; for instance, the word 'Delta' is still used to describe the triangle of fertile land with its apex at ancient Memphis, near modern Cairo, and its base on the Mediterranean coast; the origin of the word 'pyramid' has been much discussed and it may well be that the Greek word which means 'wheaten cake' was used by them to represent the shape of the pyramid, as the word *obeliskos* means a 'little spit' or 'skewer' and 'hieroglyph' is Greek for 'sacred carving'.[7]

Some of the early Egyptologists, such as Gardiner Wilkinson,[8] with their newly acquired knowledge of the ancient Egyptians following the decipherment of hieroglyphs were condescending about Herodotus. They pointed out that he gave a great deal of inaccurate information about the Pharaohs. The Egyptologists con‑ sidered that as he had been there at a time when the priests of the temples could have correctly interpreted all the inscriptions, Herodotus would have saved everyone a great deal of time and trouble and hard work if he had given precise and detailed infor‑ mation. Herodotus states, for instance (chapter 100), that a temple librarian read to him from a papyrus a list of three hundred and thirty‑ one kings, but he was so little interested that he did not even make a note of any of the names. Manetho, the Egyptian priest who wrote a history of Egypt in Greek giving lists of kings, did not produce his work until a century and a half after Herodotus' visit; Egypto‑ logists of today[9] have had to rely on this list, handed down in a very garbled form, and on such lists as that on the Turin Papyrus dating from the time of Ramesses II (*c.* 1300 or 1200 BC) which was discovered in the nineteenth century.

There is still dispute about the number of Pharaohs and the length of some of their reigns, but it is unfair to blame Herodotus. He wrote his account of Egypt, as he states himself, from memory and he gave us something in many ways more valuable than exact information, as did William Kinglake who claimed that his *Eothen* was free from all display of sound learning and from useful statistics. Herodotus was amongst the first to describe 'one of the greatest and most singular civilizations that has ever existed' and his account 'dominated the world for more than two thousand years'.[10] His picture, for instance, of an unchanging civilization became the image of Egypt to succeeding generations; 'the Egyptians', he wrote, 'adhere to their own national customs and adopt no foreign usages'. This sense of tradition appealed to Plato, who pointed out that the Egyptians understood that rules were needed for the training of young citizens 'habituated to forms and strains of virtue'. These rules, wrote Plato in *The Laws*, the Egyptians 'fixed, and exhibited the patterns of them in their temples, and no painter or artist is allowed to innovate upon them'. It is true that there is a greater variety than Herodotus or Plato allowed for, but this emphasis on tradition has been borne out by the inscriptions and papyrus writings. 'Here we find exemplified', writes Sir Alan Gardiner, 'one of the most characteristic traits of the Egyptian habit of mind, the extraordinary attachment to the traditional as opposed to the actual, in fact a conservation of expression without parallel elsewhere in the world.' Herodotus' description of the Egyptians as gloomy was also handed on; but that was not their real nature – 'the Egyptologist knows that never was there a race more fond of life, more lighthearted or more gay'.[11]

Herodotus obtained answers, some correct and some incorrect, to questions which are still asked today. Why, for instance, did the Nile come down in flood in the heat of summer, whereas in every other country the rivers flooded in winter ? Where did all the water come from ? What was the origin of the Egyptians ? In answering such questions he depended on earlier accounts which are lost, on Greek merchants, mercenaries, and inn-keepers, and on Egyptian interpreters or dragomen, who told him the traditional stories as do dragomen today, or translated into Greek conversations he had with Egyptian priests. He was a highly accomplished reporter with no prejudices against foreigners; indeed, Plutarch later attacked him for being a friend to barbarians.

THE NILE AND THE ORIGIN OF THE EGYPTIANS

When Herodotus arrived in August the Nile was in flood; 'the country', he wrote, 'is converted into a sea, and nothing appears but the cities, which look like islands in the Aegean. At this season boats no longer keep to the course of the river, but sail right across the plain. On the voyage from Naucratis[12] to Memphis at this season, you pass close to the pyramids, whereas the usual course is by the apex of the Delta.' Similar descriptions of villages and palm trees appearing above the water and the population carrying on their business by boat, were given by nearly all travellers who came to Egypt in high summer until towards the end of the nineteenth century, when dams on the river began to be built.

The unusual behaviour of the Nile had been the subject of much discussion among earlier Greek writers and Herodotus quotes various theories put forward. One theory, which was accepted by the Greeks of the fifth century BC – attributed to Anaxagoras and referred to by Aristotle, Aeschylus, and Euripides – was that the Nile flood was caused by 'the melting of the snows'. This seemed inconceivable to Herodotus, since he believed that the Nile flowed from the west out of Libya, 'the hottest regions of the world', through Ethiopia into Egypt. In fact the snows on the great mountains of Central Africa help to feed the White Nile on its journey of over four thousand miles to the Mediterranean, while the heavy rains in Ethiopia feed the Blue Nile in the Ethiopian mountains nine thousand feet above sea-level. Claudius Ptolemy, who wrote his famous geography in Alexandria in AD 150, stated that the Nile rose from great lakes in Central Africa; but even as late as the middle of the nineteenth century there was disbelief in the reports of snow on the mountains of Central Africa and the source of the White Nile was not discovered until the last half of that century. But Herodotus' own theory as to how water was drawn up by the sun and then released on the 'Upper regions' is not very wide of the mark, as is shown by the expert, Mr H. E. Hirst in his book *The Nile* (pp. 4 and 255).

Herodotus also had interesting ideas on the formation of the Delta which became a subject for discussion down the centuries. 'Egypt', he wrote, 'has a soil that is black and crumbly as being alluvial and formed of the deposits brought down by the river from Ethiopia – quite different from the soil of Libya, Arabia or Syria.' In this he was correct; he realized that it was the Nile that brought fertility out of the south and he considered that without the Nile Egypt's civiliza tion would not have existed. He described Egypt in the much quoted phrase as 'an acquired country, the gift of the river'. This was much more than a reference to its fertile properties; he meant that the whole of the Delta had been built up and formed by the Nile. He wrote that all the region north of Memphis, that is the Delta, 'formed at one time a gulf of the sea'; evidence for that were the shells to be found on the hills and the salt that came from the soil. He argued that the Nile, over the centuries, brought down enough silt and detritus to push back the sea and form the Delta. He was much criticized for this theory, but the latest archaeological work on the Predynastic periods has shown it to be correct. 'The Nile Valley was already excavated nearly in its present form by the end of the Miocene, but the high sea level of the Pliocene brought the Medi terranean flooding into the depression, transforming it into a long narrow gulf, reaching as far south as Kom Ombo in Upper Egypt. Into the southern end of this flooded inlet the Nile and its tributaries continued to pour detritus, until by the end of the Pliocene it was filled almost to water level.'[13]

Man gradually pushed northwards and that man, wrote Hero dotus, was African. Pliny contradicted him, writing that the early Egyptians were Asiatic and the dispute has continued. The traveller, Dr R. R. Madden, made a special study of skulls of different Eastern races at the beginning of the nineteenth century; in Upper

Egypt he saw several thousand mummy heads and he 'opened the heads of fifty mummies'; they were all extremely narrow across the forehead and oblong in shape, like the heads of Nubians in measurement rather than like those of Copts.[14] Herodotus was correct; the original Predynastic people of Upper Egypt were 'of essentially African stock, a character always retained despite alien influence brought to bear on them from time to time'.[15]

These Predynastic Egyptians of the Badarian period seem to have led quite a civilized life. Miss Caton-Thompson and Mr Brunton excavating near the modern village of el-Hammamiya, the district of el-Badari and el-Mustagidda, discovered bracelets of ivory and horn, an exquisite carving of a head of a gazelle in bone, and ornamental combs in ivory or bone. 'Cosmetics were used by both men and women. They were kept in small ivory vases which the Badarian craftsmen carved with great skill.'[16] There were later settlements in what has been called the Naqada I strata, from the village of Upper Egypt of that name, and then a Naqada II strata. Even at this early period Egyptian art was influenced by artisans from Mesopotamia and Palestine. It was natural, therefore, that there should have been from the days of Herodotus an argument as to the origin of the Egyptians.

THE DELTA

Herodotus, however, carried his excellent theory about the formation of the Delta too far; he believed it was rising so fast that eventually the Nile would be unable to flood it. He was told by the Egyptian priests that in the days of King Moeris (Amenemhet III, 1820 BC, though Herodotus gave his date as 1350 BC) it only needed a flood of eight cubits in height (about twelve feet) to cover the Delta, whereas at the time that he was in Egypt it needed fifteen or sixteen cubits (twenty-two and a half to twenty-four feet). This led to an argument with the Egyptian priests who expressed surprise that Greece depended on rain from heaven and pointed out how wretchedly hungry the Greeks might one day be if there were no rain. That might be true, argued Herodotus, 'but if the country north of Memphis, that is the Delta, continues to increase in height at the rate at which it has risen in times gone by, how will it be possible for the inhabitants of that region to avoid hunger, when they will certainly have no rain, and the river will not be able to overflow their cornlands ?'

It is true that the Delta has been steadily rising for thousands of years. It is estimated that during the high flood in September the Nile carries down eight cubic yards of silt per second from Ethiopia and that the Delta had been increased by three or four feet every thousand years; some calculations make it a good deal more than this. There are also indications that the Nile flood was higher in, for instance, 2500 BC, when records sculptured on the rocks at Semna, between the Second and Third Cataract, show that the Nile flooded twenty-four feet higher than it did at the beginning of this century. Herodotus, however, made the mistake of not taking into account that the silt made the bed of the river rise even higher than the surrounding country in the Delta following its flooding, so that there was no question of the land being left uncovered, except during very low floods.

The importance attached to having early warning of a high or low river is shown by the fact that recordings on the rocks of the river-side have been discovered going as far back as 3600 BC; there are remains of ancient gauges at Semna, Aswan, Philae, Edfu, and Esna and a good deal later there was the Nilometer at Roda Island, Cairo, which still exists; 'they take the low of the Nile by certain scales', but these were not 'in the pyramid' as Shakespeare wrote. There are now about fourteen gauges as far south as Lake Victoria Nyanza. The average rise of the water was about twenty-six feet at Aswan and twenty-three feet at Cairo; it only took fourteen days for the flood water in September to travel from Khartum to Cairo, whereas during low water in May it took forty-two days. The lowest level at Cairo is about the middle of June and the rise continues until the maximum is reached at the beginning of October.

The Nile flood has been modified by the building of storage dams at Aswan, and at Gebel Awlia, and Semna in the Sudan, and others higher up. The High Dam will bring it even more under control. The visitor to Egypt today can only imagine the majesty of the full flood of the uncontrolled Blue Nile, tumbling down from the high plateau of Ethiopia and at Khartum joining the White Nile from the huge African reservoir of Lake Victoria Nyanza and flowing for over four thousand miles. The great river rushed through the narrow channel between the sandstone mountains of the Sudan and Upper Egypt and, spreading out over the Delta, was sucked in greedily by the parched and cracked land; the people had had warning to collect their cattle, sheep, and children seeking the high ground of their villages. The aspect of the country was entirely changed and there was water instead of dry land; the Nile brought life to the whole of Egypt and also carried death before it in its wildness. The Egyptians used to sacrifice each year to the Nile god Hapi a young virgin from a sacred barge, but the practice was abandoned as barbarous at the time of the Old Kingdom and a beautifully dressed doll was thrown into the river from a boat at an annual festival. This festival continues today in Cairo in spite of the altered circumstances with the Nile water controlled and stored.

Even in ancient times attempts were made to contain the river by high man-made banks and more work was required to bring the water up the banks to irrigate the fields; in a tomb at Thebes of 1250 BC there is a representation of a *shaduf*. Later other methods were used such as the Archimedes' screw, and today the *saqia* is much in evidence in the Egyptian fields to raise the water into new channels. Herodotus wrote that the Egyptians 'obtain the fruits of the field with less trouble than any other people in the world. . . . The husbandman waits till the river has of its own accord spread itself over the fields and withdrawn again to its bed, and then sows his plot of ground, and after sowing turns his swine into it – the swine tread in the corn – after which he has only to await the harvest.' He underestimated the amount of labour required; there are, for instance, representations of ancient Egyptians using ploughs to break the ground and at low Niles they had to raise the water over the banks to the irrigation channels. They grew wheat, vegetables, fruits, and flowers which were useful for honey since sugar-cane was not introduced until much later. The illustrations of Egyptian life in their tombs show how much they liked flowers for decorating the banquet table and wearing as necklets; the blue lotus (*Nymphaea caerulea*) grew in all the swamps, as did the papyrus plant with which they made ropes, sandals, mats, and light boats; the stalks cut in slices, laid side by side and dried made the writing material which was taken up by the Greeks and Romans and gave us the word 'paper'; with the flax the Egyptians produced their fine linen. The paintings show various kinds of African cattle, asses, sheep, pigs, geese, ducks, and fish in abundance. There was not the pressure of population on the land as developed later; in early times it is stated to have been about two million, rising to seven and a half million by the first century AD and falling to two and a half million in the eighteenth century; the population was thirty million in 1966.

When the system of watering land was changed from flooding or basin to permanent irrigation after the building of the dams, a network of canals was made throughout the country like the veins on the back of a leaf. This meant that work in the fields continued all the year round, 'caught up in a merciless round of almost industrial activity, the Fellah wears himself out like some performing animal'.[17] Then there is the formidable Egyptian sun, which inspired Akhenaten's famous and beautiful hymn. The climate is wonderful for the tourist in the winter, but the long summers are prostrating for all, especially for the Fellaheen toiling in the open for more than half the year in temperatures ranging from 85 to more than 105° Fahrenheit.

THE PARADOX OF EGYPT

The size of the population is not the kind of detail that Herodotus gives. He looked for what was strange and paradoxical, and sometimes generalized from individual incidents which he may have seen himself, such as that men crouched to relieve nature while women stood up. In his well-known chapter 35 he wrote: 'Not only is the climate different from that of the rest of the world, and the rivers unlike any other rivers, but the people also, in most of their manners and customs, exactly reverse the common practice of mankind. The women attend the markets and trade, while the men sit at home at the loom.' The idea that the Egyptian men were effeminate was taken from Herodotus by Sophocles and other Greek writers, He remarked, too, that they wrote from right to left, kneaded dough with their feet, and picked up dirt with their hands; certainly today, and probably in ancient times because of the shortage of wood, the peasants make small pies of animal dung which they leave to dry and use for fuel. 'They eat their food out of doors in the streets', he continued, 'but retire for private purposes to their houses, giving as a reason that what is unseemly, but necessary, ought to be done in secret'; as a result of archaeological research it has been shown that earth-closets were used in the Old Kingdom at Saqqara, and at Tell el Amarna in Dynasty XVIII, so that such sanitation may have been fairly widely used. 'In other countries, the priests have long hair, in Egypt their heads are shaven'; he emphasized the cleanliness of the Egyptians who removed the hair from all parts of the body; they, and those who had copied them, were the only people in the world who practised circumcision, which they did 'for the sake of cleanliness, considering it better to be cleanly than comely'. Circumcision was not confined to the priests, 'as we learn from the mummies and from the sculptures, where circumcision is made a distinctive mark between the Egyptians and their enemies; and, in later times when Egypt contained many foreign settlers, it was looked upon as a distinctive sign between the orthodox Egyptian and the stranger, or the non-conformist. . . . We find it existed at the earliest period of which any monuments remain.'[18]

RELIGION AND EMBALMING

The stately religious ceremonies depicted on the monuments and tombs, the strange gods with animal heads impressed Herodotus as they have other visitors; he considered that the Egyptians were 'religious to excess, far beyond any other race of men'. Bulls, cows, cats, dogs, crocodiles, mongoose, shrew-mice, hawks, falcons, ibis, and other animals or birds were all sacred to some god or other, and were embalmed in much the same way as human beings. Herodotus wrote:

There are a set of men in Egypt who practise the art of embalming, and making it their proper business. These persons, when a body is brought to them, show the bearers various models of corpses, made in wood, and painted so as to resemble nature. The most perfect is said to be after the manner of him whom I do not think it religious to name in connexion with such a matter [the form of Osiris]; the second is inferior to the first, and less costly; the third is the cheapest of all. All this the embalmers explain, and then ask in which way it is wished that the corpse should be prepared. The bearers tell them, and having concluded their bargain, take their departure, while the embalmers, left to themselves, proceed to their task.

He described the method of embalming and the use of myrrh, cassia, and all kinds of spices; how the body was placed in natron for seventy days, then washed and wrapped round, from head to foot, with bandages of fine linen cloth and smeared over with gum. 'In this state it is given back to the relations, who enclose it in a wooden case which they have had made for the purpose, shaped into the figure of a man. Then fastening the case, they place it in a sepulchral chamber, upright against the wall. Such is the most costly way of embalming the dead.' It was expensive but everyone who could afford it had their relatives embalmed since they believed in the resurrection of the physical body. They made a distinction between the spirit (*Ba*), which continued to live in another world, and the soul (*Ka*) which remained in the mummy waiting the day of resurrection when the two would be united; if there were no such resting-place as the mummy for the soul, there might be no After-life. 'Many of the Egyptians', wrote Diodorus Siculus, 'keep their ancestors' bodies in costly shrines, and look face to face upon those who have died many generations before they themselves were born; and accordingly, as they behold the stature of each man, the pro-portions of his body, and the lineaments of his face, they experience a strange emotion, just as if their ancestors were alive there before their eyes.'

They could not all afford shrines; many were kept in what later travellers of the eighteenth and nineteenth centuries called 'mummy pits' and it was one of the sights of Egypt to visit them. 'The walls were covered with paintings, and at the further end stood two full-length statues, male and female, dressed in very gay apparel. . . . The whole of this chamber was strewed with pieces of cloth, legs, arms and heads of mummies, left in this condition by the Arabs, who visit these places for the purpose of rifling the bodies and carrying off the bituminous substance with which they have been embalmed.'[19] The Arabic word *mumia* means 'bitumen' and it is from this that the English word is derived. The poorer classes would have been embalmed in bitumen in the time of Herodotus and this continued through Graeco-Roman times and was followed by many of the Copts after they had become Christians, but it probably ended as a general practice after the third century AD. The spices and myrrh were expensive because they came from Arabia and Somaliland (the Land of Punt) which meant a carefully prepared expedition, such as is shown in a series of delightful bas-reliefs in the Temple of Deir el-Bahri.

Herodotus is more generous than some of the other early Greek writers in admitting that the Greeks had learned many things from the Egyptians, and he himself considered that all the Greek gods were originally borrowed from Egypt. Of early times he wrote: 'Then Egypt had gods for its rulers who dwelt upon the earth with men, one being always supreme above the rest. The last of these was Horus [the younger], the son of Osiris, called by the Greeks Apollo. He deposed Typhon [Seth], and ruled over Egypt as its last god-king. Osiris is named Dionysus (Bacchus) by the Greeks' (chapter 144). The story of Osiris and Seth is among the most interesting of the ancient Egyptian mysteries dealing as it does with the death and resurrection of a god, but Herodotus was very careful not to give details and perhaps the priests had asked him not to reveal what they had told him, or perhaps they were nervous of ridicule by a free-thinking Greek. There may have been others such as Xenophanes (sixth century BC) who is reported to have chided the Egyptians about their gods: 'If you believe them to be gods, why do you weep for them; if they deserve your lamentations, why repute them to be gods?'[20] Xenophanes was, too, a scathing critic of anthropomorphism: 'Yet men imagine gods to be born, and to have raiment and voice and body, like themselves. . . . The gods of the Ethiopians are swarthy and flat-nosed, the gods of the Thracians are fair-haired and blue-eyed. . . . Even so oxen, lions and horses, if they had hands wherewith to grave images, would fashion gods after their own shapes.'

Herodotus did not scoff at the religion even though he thought they overdid things; he was especially interested in the Osiris festivals which he attended on several occasions and found them very similar to the Greek festival of Dionysus. The worship of Osiris went through various forms in Egypt. He was at first a water-god and a god of vegetation representing the fertile properties of the Nile. When the Nile receded and the fruits were gathered Osiris was said to be dead, but he was resurrected each year when the Nile brought down the fertile silt and the harvests sprang up. Then there was his brother Seth who was at first regarded as a beneficent god, but afterwards became the personification of evil and killed Osiris, who was buried at Abydos. His sister, Isis, restored Osiris to life with the help of the two gods Thoth and Horus. Osiris became 'the recognized symbol of the resurrection of the dead and the lord in whose hands was the power of immortality'.[21]

The Old Kingdom and its rather formal State religion with its funerary rites and rituals were largely reserved for the Pharaoh and the nobility, but the later Pyramid Texts set out magical spells and incantations which could be used by non-royal persons to protect themselves and their families from the dangers of the Other World. During the Middle Kingdom there was a 'democratization of the Hereafter' and the story of Osiris became extremely popular; each year thousands of pilgrims used to attend the Osiris festival at Abydos, and at other places, where his death, burial, and resurrection were re-enacted, and the pilgrims were able to associate themselves with the immortal properties of the god by setting up a funerary stela in the sacred enclosure of the sanctuary. The Syrians, too, had the myth of a dying god, but it was based on the sun rather than on a river.

MENES, THE FIRST PHARAOH OF A UNITED KINGDOM
Herodotus wrote that Men or Menes was the first Pharaoh to rule a

united Egypt, which fact was later supported by Manetho in his list of Pharaohs, by the Turin Papyrus, and by the Palermo Stone. Herodotus also recounted, on the authority of the priests of Memphis, how Menes diverted the River Nile and made a dike to protect the city of Memphis which he built southwest of the present city of Cairo across the river from the ancient stone quarries of Tura. He also built 'the temple of Vulcan [Ptah] which stands within the city, a vast edifice, very worthy of mention'. Of this temple that Herodotus saw hardly anything remains. Herodotus' account of Memphis fits with what Egyptologists have discovered. The city was at first called the 'White Wall' either because white was the national colour of the Kingdom of Upper Egypt and it was intended by this name to celebrate the victory of the south over the north, or because of the white gesso which covered its mud-brick walls. The Pharaoh, Phiops I, of Dynasty VI (c. 2345–2181 BC), called his pyramid at South Saqqara 'Memphis', and this name was later given to the city. Situated as it was at the junction of Upper and Lower Egypt, Memphis was well placed for administering the newly unified King-dom.[22] 'The removal of the royal residence from somewhere in the south to this admirably situated position at the apex of the Delta must be viewed as a direct consequence of the establishment of the double kingdom . . . the momentous achievement which in the eyes of the Egyptians marked the beginning of human history. A remembrance of it is found in the words "Union of Upper and Lower Egypt; circumambulation of the wall[s]" by which, alike on the Palermo Stone and elsewhere the first year of each king was characterized.'[23] It was a momentous achievement because the unity of the two Egypts meant that full use could be made of the waters of the Nile and the irrigation of the country be properly planned. Unity was also important for the defence of a flat country from the Nubians and Ethiopians to the south, from the Libyans to the west, and from the peoples of western Asia to the east and northeast. Throughout their history Egyptians have striven to maintain this unity of Upper and Lower Egypt, and to give themselves further protection by trying to control Syria and the Sudan.

Egyptologists have discovered that there was at least one earlier king before Menes, but he did not unite Upper and Lower Egypt; his name is not known but he was represented by a scorpion and is called the 'Scorpion King'. Then the name of Narmer came to light and in 1897 a votive object was discovered in the Temple of Hieraconopolis of what became known as the famous Palette of Narmer, now in the Cairo Museum; it was realized that it belonged to the latest of what were called 'Predynastic times'. On one side of the Palette the King wears the White Crown of Upper Egypt and on the other side the Red Crown of Lower Egypt, and Narmer has been identified by Egyptologists with Menes, the first king to unite the two lands; the dates of Dynasty I are now given as *c.* 3100–2890 BC. These early kings, or Pharaohs, were closely associated with the gods Horus of Nekhen and Seth of Ombas (Naqada); in early days Seth was a beneficent divinity. The kings were regarded as themselves divine and the State was organized on the basis of this doctrine, which included a code of behaviour for the King and the right of succession was passed on through the Queen. Evidence suggests that there was contact in these early times between Egypt and the Syrian coast and that there were Mesopotamian influences in the arts probably due to the migration of Sumerians to the Nile Valley.

THE PYRAMIDS OF GIZA

On the high plateau of Giza, south of Cairo, nearly one hundred feet above the Nile Valley, stand majestically one of the Seven Wonders of the World – the Pyramids of Cheops, Chephren, and Mycerinus; these names were given by Herodotus and have been retained although they are not the names in the hieroglyphs. The Great Pyramid of Cheops (Khufu) had been built about eighty years after Djoser's Step Pyramid at Saqqara and had been in existence for more than two thousand years when Herodotus visited it.[24] Much of the outer casing, which has now disappeared, was left and on it were 'inscriptions in Egyptian characters on the pyramid telling how much was spent on radishes, onions and garlic for the workmen, and if I remember rightly what the interpreter told me when he read me the inscriptions, they cost a thousand and six hundred talents of silver'. This list was more likely to have been the offerings required by the dead Cheops for his well-being in the Other World. On the east side of the Pyramid was a 'false door' which enabled the dead Pharaoh to come forth and receive the food from the various estates which formed part of the funerary foundation. Boats were found buried by the Pyramids enabling the Pharaoh to travel where he wished as he had during his life.

Herodotus describes the causeway, which led from the valley temple up to the Pyramid temple, as being covered with polished and dressed stone decorated with reliefs which have disappeared. The causeway, which was originally roofed over, was the processional route for the priests to bring offerings from the temple on the Nile to the King in his Pyramid. Herodotus' interpreter was at fault in stating that the object of the causeway was to bring the blocks of stone for the Pyramid. Only in the last sixty years or so of excavations has it been realized that the Pyramid was not an independent tomb on its own but 'rather as a culminating point of a vast funerary area'. The valley temple at the bottom of the causeway was reached by boat in the period of inundation. Herodotus himself came directly by boat from Naucratis in the north to the foot of the plateau on which stand the Pyramids. All the buildings, including the Pyramid, were made attractive with reliefs and inscriptions which had religious significance, describing the ritual to be carried out in honour of the Pharaoh and describing his great achievements. These were the reliefs, or some of them, seen by Herodotus.

The smaller pyramids belonged to wives of the royal family, for it was only royalty who were allowed to have the pyramid shape for their tombs; princes and the most distinguished of the nobles and courtiers were allowed the flat-topped mastabas. These tombs were in orderly lines and looked like a small town of the dead built round the Pharaoh's Pyramid.

Herodotus gives the length of the causeway and the measurements of the Great Pyramid as have others after him, but these convey little idea of their awe-inspiring size, especially if seen at dawn or dusk, nor does it signify a great deal to say that it is the largest building of

27

stone ever raised by man. Herodotus' reaction was to think of all the wretched Egyptians who had had to build it and, indeed, the stories told to him made out that Cheops was a wicked Pharaoh. 'He made all the Egyptians work for him. Some were required to drag blocks of stone down to the Nile from the quarries in the Arabian range [the quarries of Tura]; others received the blocks after they had been conveyed in boats across the river hauling them to the mountains called Libyan. One hundred thousand men at a time worked for three months.' That was probably each year during the Nile inunda- tion when the people were not needed in the fields and it was possible to transport the heavy blocks by water. Herodotus states that it took ten years to build the causeway and the underground chambers for the King's burial and twenty years to build the Pyramid itself. 'This pyramid', he wrote, 'was built after the manner of steps, which some call "ramparts" and others "altar steps". When this first stage of the construction had been completed, the remaining stones were raised by means of contrivances of short logs of wood, being lifted first from the ground to the first tier of the steps, and from there to a second engine erected on the first tier of the steps . . .' (chapters 124–5). It looked at first, therefore, very much like one of the step pyramids, but the steps were then filled in with stones and a smooth outer casing of stone put on. This account is the fullest that has survived of labour in early times. Sir Flinders Petrie considered that it fitted conditions closely, but he did not think that the Egyptians suffered.

> Much nonsense has been written about the oppression of the people, their tears and groans. With the splendid organization evident in the work, the people must have been well managed, and there was no hardship whatever in carrying out the work. Each man might be levied twice in his lifetime; he would be just as well off there as at home, for he could do nothing during the inunda- tion. . . . The immense gain to the people was the education in combined work and technical training.[25]

It is possible that they did not appreciate these advantages; but the Egyptians were, politically and socially, a very conventional and obedient people. It was an efficient and well-organized bureaucratic system and great importance was attached to promotion in it. Herodotus, however, was sure that there must have been great suffering judging by the stories he was told, some of which read like *The Thousand and One Nights*:

> The wickedness of Cheops reached such a pitch, that being in want of money, he prostituted his daughter and ordered her to make a certain sum of money; but I was not told how much. This she did, and being secretly minded also to provide for her own memorial, she demanded of every man that lay with her the gift of one stone towards it. And of these stones, they say, was built the midmost of the three pyramids, fronting the great pyramid, whose sides are a hundred and fifty feet long.[26]

The three small pyramids on the eastern side of the Great Pyramid were intended for Cheops' royal wives. It was on the east side of the Great Pyramid that the Harvard Expedition directed by Dr Reisner in February 1925, discovered at the bottom of a carefully concealed tomb shaft one hundred feet in depth the funerary equipment of the mother of Cheops and the wife of Snofru, Queen Hetepheres. This beautiful furniture is in the Cairo Museum – the Queen's carrying-chair, her gold-encased bed, gold toilet requisites, an arm-chair, and other objects. 'The costly materials and refinement of design of these beautiful objects give us a startling glimpse of the wealth and good taste of the time. There is the same sense of form and clean line which is embodied in the reliefs, the portrait sculpture and the funerary architecture of the period.'[27]

Herodotus considered that Chephren was almost as bad as Cheops for 'like him he built a pyramid, though of a lesser size. I myself measured it.' There is little Egyptological evidence about Cheops except that he was pious and built temples and was something of an autocrat, whereas his father, Snofru, is stated to have been a friendly and genial character, even though he probably owned three Pyramids. There is no doubt that they were all very strong on the personality cult, after death as well as in life, which became less popular later; but in those days Egyptians believed their Pharaoh was a god. At the same time the Pharaoh was not allowed to be an irresponsible tyrant. 'He was held in', wrote Sir Flinders Petrie, 'by being part of a highly organized official machinery, in which everyone knew their own business, and his official acts were part of that machinery; as to his private life, even that was not his own, but he had to act every hour according to fixed routine, without room for the licence of a Dionysius or a Caligula. . . . The political position of the king was that of successor to several separate States, each of which was probably tenacious of its rights, and thus a series of obligations were combined in the royal position.' The famous Maxims of the Vizier Ptahhotep, who lived in Dynasty V (c. 2494–2345 BC), expressed a very civilized view of correct behaviour, describing the main virtues as obedience to a father and a superior, tact, good manners, and general humility.

There were numerous highly skilled artists, sculptors, engineers, artisans, and craftsmen whose work was so good that they must have taken pleasure in it. Considerable engineering skill was needed to build the Pyramids and the elaborately contrived corridors within to foil the tomb robbers showed great ingenuity. From the earliest times there had been tomb robberies, sometimes even before the tombs were properly closed. In Snofru's Pyramid at Saqqara the entrance was high up on the face and the door looked like any of the other copingstones. In the Pyramids of Cheops and of Chephren the same principle was followed and the exits from the burial chamber were closed after the work had been completed. Herodotus states that there was a waterfilled moat round the Cheops' burial chamber, but there is no confirmation of this. Mycerinus, the builder of the third and smallest of the three main Pyramids at Giza, had portcullises across the passageways but these were undermined. Fortunately, there has survived undamaged the wonderful lifesize slate statue of Mycerinus and his Queen which is in the Boston Museum.

Life for the Egyptians at the time of Cheops and Chephren was almost certainly not as bad as is made out in the stories which were told to Herodotus. These may very well have reflected the unhappy state of the Egyptians in a later period, such as Dynasty VI which ended in a whole series of weak kings, or even the later times of the occupation of Lower Egypt by a people from western Asia, known as the Hyksos period. In those times there grew up a pessimistic literature with the refrain that it was useless to build elaborate tombs when they were robbed and destroyed:

> Behold the places thereof
> Their walls are dismantled
> Their places are no more,
> As if they had never been.
> None cometh from thence
> That he may tell how they fare.

INFLUENCE OF THE PYRAMIDS

This remarkable people, who had a profound effect on the civilization of the ancient Greeks, have certainly exerted an influence on the Egyptians of today; the Pyramids of Giza, for instance, are a constant reminder to the citizens of Cairo of their heritage. 'Ours is the oldest of civilizations. Our ancestors have handed down to us undisputed social virtues . . . [stated the Egyptian nationalist leader, Saad Zaghlul, demanding independence in 1919]. To ask a nation like this whether it is agreed on independence is an affront to it.' He was certainly thinking of the heritage from the ancient Egyptians. The Egyptian biographer of Saad Zaghlul (1936) took it for granted that there was an identity between ancient and modern Egyptians and referred to the Arabs as foreign invaders.

The building of the Great Pyramid of Giza is a theme in an interesting novel called *The Rebirth* or *The Rediscovered Soul* (1933), written by the well-known Egyptian playwright, Tawfik al-Hakim. In this he described the Egyptian Revolution of 1919 and went back to the ancient Egyptians to explain the suddenness and spontaneity of the explosion among the Fellaheen, which took the British and the Egyptian leaders themselves by surprise. In the novel, Fouquet, an archaeologist, is talking to a British inspector called Black while they watch Fellaheen at work in the fields before the 1919 Revolution. 'Beware of this people', states Fouquet, 'because it carries within itself a tremendous spiritual power.' Black expresses scepticism as he watches them peaceably labouring, and Fouquet continues:

We may be excused if we do not understand. For our language – we Europeans – is the language of sensual things. We cannot imagine the impulses which once made of this people one single person, able to carry on its shoulders for twenty years those huge rocks, with a smile on its lips and joy in its heart, content with pain for the sake of the worshipped one. Those thousands upon thou- sands of people who built the pyramids could not have been forcibly driven to work, as Herodotus has stupidly suggested. On the contrary, they flocked to work singing the hymns of the wor- shipped one in the same way as their descendants do at present in harvest time. . . . This collective joy and pain, this feeling of beautiful patience, of gay endurance of sufferings for the sake of a common cause, this feeling of faith for the worshipped one . . . this is their strength and power.

Black does not consider that there is any relationship between the ancient and present-day Egyptians, but Fouquet is insistent that the age-old spiritual force is latent and only needs the appearance of 'the Worshipped One' from the ranks of the people – by whom he meant Saad Zaghlul – to bring about 'another miracle like that of the pyramids'.[28]

EGYPTIANS OR ARABS?

Egyptians have for some time been faced by the problem whether to think in terms of territorial nationalism confined to Egypt, or to consider themselves as part of the other Arab countries in a wider Arab nationalism as heirs to their great Arab civilization. When the alien concept of nationalism was first imported from Europe at the beginning of the nineteenth century, an Egyptian Azharite wrote a history of Egypt from Pharaonic times to the Arab Conquest and took a pride in the glories of ancient Egypt. A Rector of Cairo University wrote that there was no danger of European civilization engulfing Egyptians since there existed already a strong Egyptian personality going back to the Pharaohs, and when world interest was aroused in the discovery of the tomb of Tutankhamen in 1923, there was a wave of 'pharaonism' among Egyptian writers.

The concept of Arabism, however, remained strong and is especially strong today, through Islam and the Arabic language which is spoken from the Atlantic seaboard of Morocco to the Persian Gulf, in a great part of western Asia and south to the Sudan. President Gamal Abdel Nasser, for political reasons, decided that to meet the threat of European and American imperialism Egypt must take the lead and strengthen the 'Arab circle'.

The question remains, are they Egyptians or are they Arabs? A modern Egyptian writer has pointed out that at the time of the Arab conquest of Egypt there was little intermarriage between the Arab invaders and the Egyptians of the country-side and that 'Egyptians have more or less preserved the characteristics of their Pharaonic ancestors'; he considered that that was due to the fact that rural Egypt had always been the main reservoir feeding the cities with inhabitants.

With the exception of the Arab conquerors, foreigners coming to Egypt settled in the cities. The Arab conquerors were not settlers at all, they were Bedouin tribes who lived and still live in tents in the outskirts of the valley. They had blood theories and nomadic habits which kept them from intermarriage with the Fellaheen. Only the aristocracy – the army generals and the tribe leaders who came in the wake of the conquest – settled in the cities to trade. . . . With each invasion, the influx of foreign blood would alter the Egyptian physiognomy in the cities, but with succeeding generations of emigrants from rural districts, the foreign characteristics became submerged and the national type once more predominated.[29]

That is true; the Egyptians, especially of the country-side, have today a greater homogeneity in physique and ways of thought than neighbouring populations in Syria, Jordan, and Lebanon. It should be added, however, that although Muslim women were not allowed to marry non-Muslims, more and more Copts under later persecutions became Muslim and more Arabs migrated from Arabia to Egypt during the centuries; this meant that there was considerable

33

Arabization of the population and yet on the whole it retained its distinctive Egyptian characteristics.[30]

Egypt, therefore, is heir to two major civilizations, that of ancient Egypt and of the Arab civilization of Mecca, Damascus, and Baghdad. 'We are not a nation to be despised', wrote Dr Lufti al-Sayyed. 'Twice in the history of the world we gave birth to civilization and preserved it.' To be heirs to two great civilizations can produce difficulties and there are other influences of which account must be taken – the period when Ptolemaic Alexandria was the capital of Egypt, and the period of Christian Egypt which lasted until the Muslim Conquest.

2   Alexandria the capital city

'The City was all white and bright by night as well as by day.'

Alexander the Great was no more than a visitor to Egypt even though he came as a conqueror, but he is still remembered in Egyptian folk-lore. He arrived when he was twenty-five years old after defeating the Persians and stayed long enough to visit Memphis, return to the coast, and to choose the site for a Greek city at Rhakotis, which was to be the capital of his newly acquired Egyptian kingdom and a link across the Mediterranean with Macedonia. He had time to make a hurried journey to Siwa Oasis, two hundred miles into the Western Desert, where in the Temple of Ammon the Egyptian priests pro-claimed him Pharaoh and a god. From there Alexander hurried on to complete his defeat of the Persian Empire. He reached the Indus Valley and returned to Babylon on the Euphrates where he died of malaria at the age of thirty-three, one of the greatest and most romantic figures of history. His body was brought to Memphis for burial but, according to the legend, the High Priest objected: 'Do not settle him here, but at the city he has built at Rhakotis, for where-ever this body lies the city will be uneasy, disturbed with wars and battles.' Wrapped in gold and in a glass sarcophagus Alexander journeyed down the Nile to be buried in the centre of his city which had progressed during the eight years of his absence; his body was never discovered and it was for a long time believed that it lay under the present Mosque of the Prophet Daniel.

THE PTOLEMIES
Alexander's Empire was divided among his generals and Egypt

35

fell to the lot of Ptolemy who became known as Ptolemy Soter; the dynasty lasted from 323 BC to about 30 BC and the rulers were pro/ claimed Pharaohs. Alexandria became the capital of Egypt and one of the first capitals in the world attracting merchants, sea/cap/ tains, philosophers, and mathematicians. Pompey's Pillar, which stands today, marks the site of the Citadel of the ancient Egyptian city of Rhakotis, which may date back to Seti I (1350 BC). Ptolemy Soter decided that the Greeks must have their own god and com/ bined Osiris with the bull cult of Apis at Memphis, calling the god 'Serapis'; a huge temple was built known as the 'Serapeum'. The building called the 'Mouseion' contained the famous library, lecture halls, laboratories, observatories, and a zoo, and there was the huge palace area in the neighbourhood of Silsileh. Where Fort Kait Bey now stands was a building which attracted many visitors – the great lighthouse, or Pharos, known as one of the Seven Wonders of the World.

This great city of shining marble and limestone built by the blue Mediterranean attracted many talented men from Greece, who found what they needed for their scientific studies in the Mouseion building. The architect Sostratus carefully worked out the measurements of the huge lighthouse, Euclid composed his *Elements* in Alexandria, Eratosthenes worked at the observatory and proclaimed that the earth was round, Aristarchus of Samos reasoned out that the earth revolved round the sun, Erasistratus argued that there was a con/ nexion between sex and nervous troubles, and there were many other philosophers, poets, mathematicians, astronomers, and geographers.

Alexandria grew into a vast city of two nations, Greeks and Egyptians, each speaking their own languages and worshipping their own gods in a remarkably tolerant atmosphere; indeed, the Ptolemies continued to repair various Egyptian temples throughout the country, cleared an ancient canal from the Nile to the Red Sea, and founded the town of Berenice. It was not until the Christians came that the idea was propagated that there was only one true religion and that others were false. The Ptolemy rulers adopted many Egyptian ways such as marrying their sisters and keeping the high estate which had been maintained by earlier Pharaohs. The country was at first well governed, trade with India and Rome was active, and the people were on the whole contented, at any rate under the first three Ptolemies, but after that the rulers were weak and there were revolts in Thebes and elsewhere.

The Greeks who arrived in large numbers were either interested in their astronomy, philosophy, and various sciences or they were merchants who were not interested in writing about the country. It is not until Diodorus Siculus, the Greek author and traveller, arrived in Egypt in about 59 BC that any attempt was made to describe the country and the religion since the time of Herodotus. He covered much the same ground but not as well or as entertainingly. In Book I of his *General History* Diodorus Siculus shows great interest in the Osiris myth and described how the Pharaoh's life is regulated according to ritual; he gave an account of the laws, education, animal worship, and admits the debt that the Greeks owed to Egypt. The Romans began to be interested in Egypt as a potentially useful and attractive colony and it was argued that Ptolemy X had bequeathed his kingdom to them. Pompey after his defeat by Julius Caesar at Pharsalus in 48 BC decided to take refuge in Egypt but was murdered by one of his centurions as he was landing. Julius Caesar only learned of this on arrival in Alexandria in pursuit of Pompey.

During this period Cleopatra had become Queen of Egypt in 51 BC at the age of seventeen. Her brother and husband, Ptolemy XIV, was ten years old, and she had tried to get rid of him but was herself ousted from the palace. She was a shrewd and capable woman who knew the Egyptian language as well as Greek and it is argued by some that she was anxious to regain the throne not only for her own sake but also for patriotic reasons – to maintain some independence for Egypt against the powerful Romans; she considered that it was only by winning over their leaders that she could gain her ends. She smuggled herself to Julius Caesar and won his support against her brother, who was in Egyptian eyes the Pharaoh of Egypt. Caesar had hurried ahead of his main body of troops in order to deal with Pompey and was not in a strong position when the Egyptians rose against the small force of Romans. There was a series of naval and land engagements in which Caesar nearly lost his life; it is believed that it was at this time that the great library in the Mouseion was destroyed. With the arrival of reinforcements Caesar defeated the Egyptians and Ptolemy XIV disappeared, but Cleopatra became Queen again by marrying her younger brother who became Ptolemy XV.

Julius Caesar travelled up the Nile with Cleopatra, visiting the ancient monuments. She later bore him a son called Caesarion. Cleopatra followed Julius Caesar to Rome where she lived openly as his mistress until he was assassinated in 44 BC. She then returned to Egypt, regretting perhaps that she had attached herself to the wrong man. In the battle between Caesar's assassins and Mark Antony she remained neutral, but when Mark Antony obtained the control of Egypt and the Eastern provinces Cleopatra made it her business to win him. The story of Antony and Cleopatra became a legend; Plutarch romanticized it and Shakespeare turned it into poetry. 'Voluptuous but watchful', wrote E. M. Forster, 'she treated her new lover as she had treated her old. She never bored him, and since grossness means monotony she sharpened his mind to those more delicate delights, where sense verges into spirit. Her infinite variety lay in that. She was the last of a secluded and subtle race, she was a flower that Alexandria had taken three hundred years to produce and that eternity cannot wither, and she unfolded herself to a simple but intelligent Roman soldier.'[31] Cleopatra bore him a number of children, had Antony proclaimed a god, and built a temple which became known as the 'Caesareum'. There she had erected two obelisks which came from Heliopolis originally placed there by Thutmosis III of Dynasty XVIII (c. 1500 BC); one of these is now on the Thames Embankment in London and the other in New York.

Antony and Cleopatra were defeated at the Battle of Actium and there arrived Julius Caesar's nephew, Octavian, 'one of the most odious of the world's successful men and to his cold mind the career of Cleopatra could appear as nothing but a vulgar debauch'. After the suicide of Antony and Cleopatra Alexandria ceased to be in touch with the vigorous life of Greece. Rome extended her power over her and the rest of Egypt for the next two hundred years, 'legal and self-righteous, she struck a chill into the whole Hellenistic world. She was horrified at the corruption – a corruption of which she never failed to take advantage.' The rule of the Ptolemies came to an end. Greek though it was, the dynasty 'did represent the complex country that it ruled. In Upper Egypt it carried on the traditions of the Pharaohs: on the coast it was Hellenistic and in touch with Mediterranean culture. After its extinction, the vigour of Alexandria turned inwards. She is to do big things in philosophy and religion. But she is no longer the capital of a kingdom, no longer royal.' She became one of the great centres of Christianity.

MAN'S RELATIONS WITH GOD

The Jews had for some time been emigrating in large numbers to Alexandria from Palestine; they came to form a third nation alongside the Greeks and Egyptians, which added to strife in the city. The younger generations of Jews learned to speak only Greek, and the Hebrew Scriptures had to be translated for their benefit; this was the Septuagint version, completed c. 130 BC. The Greek philosophers and the Jews were much concerned with the question of God's relations with man; they did not want God to be too indefinite and far away, but at the same time there were complications if they made him too close, so they sought for some intermediate link. Philo, the most important exponent of Hellenistic-Judaism, tried to make the concept of the Jewish Jehovah more comprehensible by introducing the link of the 'Logos' or 'Word'; his philosophy may have suggested the opening of St John's Gospel 'In the beginning was the Word... and the Word was God'. The Christians of Alexandria were influenced by this love for discussion and the desire to find a rational basis for beliefs and ideas; this was to lead to terrible confusion and strife when it came to defining the nature of Christ.

THE SPREAD OF CHRISTIANITY

The spread of Christianity in Egypt and northwards into the Sudan and to Ethiopia started from Alexandria. St Mark, the traditional

39

author of the Second Gospel, is reputed to have come there in about AD 45 and to have founded his church where he used to preach; there is also a legend that he was martyred in Alexandria, though others say he died a natural death; and there was the further legend, none of which is likely to be true, that his body was removed from Alexandria to Venice in the ninth century concealed in a barrel of pork to discourage the Muslim officials in the harbour of Alexandria from prying.

Christianity was influenced by the teaching of the followers of Plato; his reasoning that the world was an imperfect copy of an ideal world was pushed by the ascetics to the conclusion that the present world was of no importance. This led the blameless Origen to emasculate himself to avoid the lusts of the flesh, influenced per-haps by the reference in St Matthew's Gospel (xix, 12) 'and there be eunuchs who have made themselves eunuchs for the kingdom of heaven's sake'. Christianity was also influenced by the traditional beliefs and cults of ancient Egypt, which made the new religion more understandable to the Egyptian masses and less coldly abstract.

Hadrian, Roman Emperor from AD 117 to 138, spent some years in Egypt, and wrote cynically to a friend, 'those who call themselves followers of Christ pay their devotions to Serapis. The Patriarch himself whenever he goes into Egypt is obliged by some to worship Serapis, by others Christ.' The Roman Emperor was impressed by the wealth of Alexandria 'without an idle inhabitant' – they made glass, paper, and linen, and he reported that every description of artisan could be hired. He travelled up the Nile with his wife Sabina and a party went to listen at dawn to the 'music' from the statue of 'Memnon'. On the first occasion no sound was heard and the Emperor expressed his displeasure, so that on the second visit the Egyptian priests made sure that there was no disappointment.

Where the Greeks had taught philosophy in Alexandria there was now a theological college. Under the tolerant Bishop Clement of Alexandria the Greek sciences were studied as well as the Holy Scriptures and Clement sought in his writings to reconcile the two. Christ, he argued, had existed from the time of the Creation and all that had gone before was in preparation for the time that He should come down to earth as the link between God and man.

THE NATURE OF CHRIST: ARIANISM

That was satisfactory as far as it went, but the Alexandrians insisted on taking things further and defining the nature of Christ. Christ being the Son of God, argued Arius, must be younger and could not have existed from all time; this creed of Arianism was very popular because it brought Christ nearer to man. It was violently opposed, however, by the orthodox Greek Church of Constantinople which confirmed at the Council of Nicaea (AD 325) that Arianism was heretical.

From c. AD 200 there were a series of terrible persecutions of the Christians by Roman Emperors, some of whom were pagan or had been influenced by the Arian heresy; the end of the third century and the beginning of the fourth became known as the 'Era of Martyrs' when Egyptian men and women in hundreds chose death to a renunciation of their faith. Thousands, who managed to escape to the Libyan or Sinai deserts, went into monasteries or caves in the hillsides. Persecution spread the faith and enraged the monks. Some of them, such as the Egyptians St Antony (b. AD 250) and St Ammon, were contemplative anchorites and caused no trouble except to their families whom they refused to see; but the majority were a wild, barefoot, black-clothed army of irregulars, who were filled with a passion to destroy the pagan temples or convert them to Christian use. When Constantine adopted Christianity as the religion of the Roman Empire in the fourth century, their power was increased. It is estimated that out of six million Egyptians, four million were Christian.

Egypt was ruled from Constantinople, the ancient town of Byzantium, chosen by Constantine as the capital of the Eastern Roman Empire in AD 330 instead of Alexandria, which would have been the natural capital, but there was too much confusion and controversy. According to Edward Gibbon the Egyptians had treated the new religion with coldness and even in the time of Origen (AD 185–254) 'it was rare to meet with an Egyptian who had surmounted his early prejudice in favour of the sacred animals of his country', but as soon as Christianity became the accepted religion 'the cities of Egypt were filled with Bishops, and the deserts of Thebais swarmed with hermits'. He gives a fascinating account in *The Decline and Fall of the Roman Empire* of the vexed question of the Christian controversies and of their persecution by the Romans, by the Greeks of Constantinople, and by each other, but his cynicism is not always to the liking of orthodox Christians such as Mrs E. L. Butcher who wrote *The Story of the Church of Egypt*.

THE NATURE OF CHRIST: SINGLE OR DUAL?

The second great controversy which wracked the Christian Church also concerned the nature of Christ. He was the Son of God but also the Son of Mary; did He have two natures or one? The Egyptian Christians declared firmly that He had one nature, which was called Monophysism, but the Council of Chalcedon in AD 451 maintained the orthodox definition, which is retained today, that Christ has two natures and was at once both God and man. This decision was of great importance to Egypt for the condemnation of the Monophysite doctrine led to schism and repeated conflicts. The Egyptian Patriarch Dioscorus was exiled from Egypt by decision of the Council of Chalcedon and the Egyptian Christians revolted at this treatment of their favourite and set up their own Patriarch.

The racial issue as between Greek and Egyptian, which the Ptolemies had managed to control, broke out with great violence against the 'foreigner', so that for some time no Greek could count on being secure in Egypt. There were now two Christian Patriarchs; one was orthodox and Greek, appointed by the Emperor at Constantinople, who had funds but little spiritual control over the people; the other was an Egyptian, who was poor but popular; each claimed to represent St Mark and the true Church. The Egyptian Christians called themselves Copts and it was to some extent a national movement. Their language was derived from that of ancient Egypt, though they made use of the Greek script with the addition of six letters from the hieroglyphs. This schism in the Church remains to this day.

42

The Egyptian Christians, who belonged to what became known as the Jacobite Church (Monophysite), lived as much as possible in their monasteries away from their orthodox Greek overlords of Constantinople, belonging to what became known as the Melkite Church. Those Egyptians, who still worshipped their ancient gods, went in fear of the barefoot monks who had destroyed various pagan buildings including the Temple of Serapis at Canopus (Abukir) and the great building of the Serapeum in the centre of Alexandria, when it is probable that the second library collected by Cleopatra was burned. In AD 415 these fierce men seized Hypatia in Alexandria on her return in her carriage from delivering a lecture on Greek philosophy, dragged her to the Christian cathedral which had been the Temple of Mark Antony, and tore her to pieces.

These rages, however, were spasmodic and most of the time they kept themselves shut up in their monasteries throughout the country, though some of them worked in the fields, collected natron, or made cloth. The enormous numbers who had retired to monasteries had aroused the interest of the Church of Rome. 'The extent to which the population became monks and nuns could hardly be believed if it were not attested by contemporary writers, who travelled to Egypt to see this strange thing for themselves.'[32] Two young Italian priests, Rufinas and Jerome, were sent in the fourth century to investigate the monastic life of Egypt for it was there that monasticism had first begun. At Oxyrhynchus (el-Bahnesa) in Upper Egypt the Italians reported that there were ten thousand monks and twenty thousand nuns; the great temples had been turned into monasteries and there were also twelve churches. With regard to a large monastery near Hermopolis it was remarked, as an unusual piece of information, 'their garments were clean as their hearts were pure'. It was, indeed, unusual. The ancient Egyptians regarded cleanliness as most important, as is shown by Herodotus, and when they became monks many of them considered that part of the penance was to give up that luxury. 'The aspect of a genuine anchorite', wrote Edward Gibbon, 'was horrid and disgusting; every sensation that is offensive to man was thought acceptable to God'; but at the same time there were many learned among them and Greek, Roman, and Church literature was 'preserved and multiplied by their indefatigable pens'.

Life in these monasteries throughout Egypt was very different to that of the ordinary peasant, whose day's work was controlled by the rhythm of the Nile and the need to produce crops required for the cities. Until the Arab Conquest in the seventh century Alexandria remained the second city of the Eastern Roman Empire after Con-stantinople, which was supplied with wheat and other crops from Egypt through the port of Alexandria, 'the seat of commerce, luxury and letters. . . . The vast population was provided in unexampled profusion with theatres, baths and places of amusement. A forest of ships congregated in its safe and spacious harbour, from whence communication was maintained with all the seaports of the world. . . . It was otherwise with the rich valley beyond. Emerging from the luxurious city, the traveller dropped at once from the pinnacle of civilization to the dreary wastes of Monasticism, and the depths of poverty and squalor. Egypt was then, as ever, the servant of nations.'[33]

THE OPPRESSION OF CYRUS

The Eastern Roman Emperor Heraclius (AD 575–642) tried to settle the doctrinal civil war in Egypt over the Monophysite faith by producing another variation called 'Monothelism', but it was only a further complication. The Emperor's willing servant, Cyrus, was sent to Egypt in AD 630 as Orthodox Patriarch and Viceroy to convert the Copts either to Monothelism or to Orthodoxy; for ten years he carried out a systematic persecution. The rival Coptic Patriarch Benjamin fled to Upper Egypt and concealed himself in a monastery, advising his followers to keep out of the way of their Greek overlords. The Egyptians were therefore in a fever of dis-content, oppressed not only in their religion but also because of the large amount of agricultural produce they had to send away. The persecution of the Emperors, wrote Gibbon, had 'converted a sect into a nation and alienated Egypt from their religion and govern-ment'.

44

1 The wall-paintings in ancient Egyptian tombs reveal much about the life and customs of the people. A wall-painting of a grape harvest in the tomb of Nakht at Thebes (Dynasty XVIII 1567–1320 BC).

2 The dead were bewailed and mummified. A wall-painting of female mourners in the tomb of Ramosi at Thebes dating from the same period.

3 (*below*) The massive stone seated figure of Ramesses II, who was one of the Pharaohs ruling Egypt for many centuries, at the temple of Abu Simbel; he belonged to Dynasty XX 1200–1085 BC.

4 (*right above*) The tombs of the Pharaohs at Giza, known as the Great Pyramids, still dominate the landscape south of Cairo. Painting by Edward Lear dated 1854.

5 (*right below*) The stone-covered causeways which led from the Valley Temple to the Pyramid were used for processions of priests bringing offerings. A reconstruction of the Pyramid field at Abusir, after a painting by Borchardt.

6 (*left above*) A rare ivory carving of the Pharaoh Cheops (Dynasty IV *c.* 2613–2494 BC) now in the Cairo Museum.

7 and 8 The Diorite statue of the seated Pharaoh Chephren (*left*) and the slate triad of Mycerinus walking between two goddesses (*above*) date from the same period.

9 At the sacred city of Karnak at Thebes the great pillared hall was built during
Dynasty XX 1200–1085 B.C.

10 The funerary temple of Deir el-Bahri was built during Dynasty XX 1200–1085 BC, at the command of Queen Hatshepsut.

11 A drawing of a bas-relief at Deir el-Bahri of the expedition to the Land of Punt (Somaliland) showing frankincese being stored for offerings in the temple.

12 (*below*) The head of King Amenemhet III (Dynasty XII 1991–1786 BC)
from a grey marble statuette of the period.

13 (*right*) The gold inlaid mummy mask
of Tutankhamen (Dynasty XVIII 1580–
1314 BC) found at his tomb in the Valley
of the Kings near Luzor.

14 (*right*) In 1897 the slate Palette belonging to King Narmer (Menes) the
first Pharaoh to unite the two Kingdoms
of Egypt was discovered. Here it shows
the king wearing the White Crown of
Upper Egypt. On the obverse side he
wears the Red Crown of Lower Egypt.

15 Alexander the Great conquered Egypt in the fourth century BC; on his death his Empire was divided among his generals and Egypt fell to the lot of Ptolemy I Soter. This Roman bronze statue now at the Naples Museum was probably made in the first century AD.

16 (*left*) In 51 BC Cleopatra be͵ came Queen of Egypt. A stone bust in the British Museum identi͵ fied as Cleopatra.

17 (*above*) The Romans were by this time expanding their Empire and after the death of Julius Caesar, Mark Antony became ruler of Egypt. A silver coin showing his head.

3   Arab invasions

WHEN THE PROPHET MOHAMMED DIED at Medina in AD 632 one of the greatest migrations in history took place: the Arabs burst out of the Arabian peninsula inspired and disciplined by the Muslim faith, defeating the experienced soldiers of the Greek and Persian Empires. Having helped in the capture of Syria from the Greeks, one of the ablest of the Arab generals, Amr, Ibn al-As, who had visited Egypt as a merchant in his pagan days, obtained the reluctant permission of the second Caliph Omar to take a force of four thousand cavalry and men from Syria for the conquest of Egypt. It was a bold venture considering the strength of such fortresses as Babylon near ancient Memphis, and of cities like Alexandria, but before Amr got into too many difficulties reinforcements arrived under the redoubtable Arab commander, Zubair.

Amr captured Pelusium in December AD 639 and in July 640 won the battle of Heliopolis. The Arabs were opposed almost entirely by Greek forces of the Eastern Roman Empire; the Copts and Nubians in Heliopolis and elsewhere saw no reason to fight the Arabs, who could not, they considered, be much worse than their Greek overlords. The fortress of Babylon was besieged for eight months, eventually on the island of Roda the Greek Viceroy, Cyrus, treated with a delegation of ten Arabs led by a renowned and power-ful Negro called Ubadah ibn as Samit. When the proud Cyrus saw him he said: 'Take away that black man: I can have no discussion with him.' The Arab delegation explained that Ubadah was one of the Commander's most trusted officers and the Viceroy was lec-tured to the effect that Muslims judged men by character and not by colour. 'I much fear', muttered Cyrus, 'that God has sent these men to devastate the world.'[34]

The Emperor Heraclius died and Babylon was captured in April AD 641. The Greek magistrates, officials, and merchants left Upper Egypt and escaped down the Nile towards Alexandria while the Greek troops delayed the advance of the Arabs at the many irrigation channels, but Amr reached Alexandria in just over three weeks. He began a siege which was to last for fourteen months and lead to the loss of several thousand Arab troops.

Alexandria was finally captured in December AD 642. 'I have taken', wrote Amr to the Caliph Omar, 'the great city of the West. It is impossible for me to enumerate the variety of its riches and beauty; and I shall content myself with observing that it contains four thousand palaces, four thousand baths, four hundred theatres or places of amusement, twelve thousand shops for the sale of vegetable food, and forty thousand tributary Jews. The town has been sub-dued by force of arms, without treaty or capitulation, and the Mus-lims are impatient to seize the fruits of their victory.' The Caliph, however, was adamant that there should be no pillaging and that the revenue should be reserved for the public service. A tribute was imposed; the Jacobite Copts and the Melkite Greek Christians were allowed to carry on their worship. The story that the Arabs destroyed the famous library of Alexandria is almost certainly incorrect.

Amr had wished to make Alexandria his capital but he was told to remain encamped on the edge of the desert because the Caliph Omar liked to feel that he could reach any of his outposts on a camel. There was wisdom in this for the Arabs with their cavalry were effective and mobile in the desert which was their home; the desert was to them what the sea became to later imperialists. The Arabs were not accustomed to irrigated lands where the rivers flooded such as Mesopotamia and Egypt. An early Arab poet wrote: 'Beware of the country of the tillers of the soil. What advantage is there in being near springs? Fever and mosquitoes consume us.'

A town of tents, known as al-Fustat, later to become the capital of Egypt, was set up near Babylon. Zubair, who had stormed the fortress of Babylon with a scaling-ladder, wanted the land divided among the Arabs as their right of conquest but Amr refused and the Caliph confirmed his decision stating 'leave it in the people's hands to nurse and fructify'. Pilgrims were coming in large numbers each year to Mecca and Medina so that the Arabs required large quantities of corn, which Egypt supplied; Amr had one of the ancient canals reopened from Upper Egypt to the Red Sea to help trade with the Hejaz. He had also proposed cutting a 'Suez Canal' but the Caliph feared that the Greek fleet might sail out of the Mediterranean into the Red Sea and attack the Hejaz. The Arabs at first had a dislike of the sea – except those who lived on the Persian or Arab Gulf – and Amr reported to the Caliph 'trust it little, fear it much; man at sea is an insect on a splinter, now engulfed, now scared to death'.

The sympathy of the Egyptians was won by Amr's refusal to shed blood unnecessarily, by his wise administration, and by his decision to conciliate the Coptic Patriarch Benjamin. He was only follow-ing the instructions of the first Caliph, Abu Bakr, who had sent instructions to his commanders in Syria, 'Avoid injustice and oppression. . . . Let not your victory be stained with the blood of women and children. . . . When you make any covenant, stand to it and be as good as your word.' He added that those who had retired into monasteries should not be molested nor the monasteries destroyed, but those who had become priests, with shaven heads, should be killed unless they became Muslims or paid tribute. Many in Egypt were converted to Islam and others paid tribute. Christians and Jews were treated better than others because they were mentioned in the Koran and were described as 'People of the Book'. Indeed, the Muslims were a great deal more tolerant to the Copts than the Copts had been to others. At that time there were independent Christian kingdoms in Nubia and the Sudan as far as the borders of Ethiopia; the Sudan had been Christian since the days of Jus-tinian (AD 483–565). The Arabs were not able at first to conquer them, due largely to the remarkable accuracy of the Nubian bowmen, famous from the time of the ancient Egyptians.

Amr gave a picturesque account of Egypt in a despatch to the

Caliph: 'O Commander of the Faithful, Egypt is a compound of black earth and green plants'. After stating that the Nile, 'rolls his swelling and sounding waters through the realm of Egypt', he wrote, rather in the manner of Herodotus:

> The retreat of the inundation deposits a fertilizing mud for the reception of the various seeds; the crowds of husbandmen who blacken the land may be compared to a swarm of industrious ants; and their native indolence is quickened by the lash of the task/ master and the promise of the flowers and fruits of a plentiful increase. Their hope is seldom deceived; but the riches which they extract from the wheat, the barley, the rice, the vegetables, the fruit trees and the cattle are unequally shared between those who labour and those who possess.

In the earlier centuries many from Arabia, Palestine, and Syria had settled in Egypt but they had adopted the manners and customs of the Egyptians. With the Arab Conquest a new civilization began, though Egyptians certainly gave their own colouring to it and retained their own characteristics. An important decision was taken in AD 706 when Arabic replaced the Coptic or Egyptian language for all official documents and for much else. The language which had been used throughout the country for from three to four thousand years, and was still spoken by Egyptians even though the Coptic Script was in Greek, was replaced by the rich and vigorous Arabic language. This was an integral part of Arab civilization, the lan/ guage of the Koran and of the Bedouin poems of love and war. 'It was the Arabization of the conquered provinces, rather than their military conquest, that is the true wonder of Arab expansion.'[35]

A PROVINCE OF THE ARAB EMPIRE

At first Egypt was part of the Arab Empire established by the Ummayyad dynasty centred on Damascus, which included western Asia, Egypt, North Africa, and Spain; throughout this large area Arabic was the official language and the peoples shared in the glories of the Arab Empire. Then came the rise of the Abbasids and Egypt was under the rule of the Caliph of Baghdad – the city founded by al-Mansur in AD 762. It was the great period of Arab civilization under the Caliph Harun al-Rashid and his son al-Mamun, who died in AD 833. There had been an exchange of presents between Harun al-Rashid and Charlemagne, but this was unusual. The early Islamic jurists maintained the concept of the Universal Sovereignty of the Caliph, so that there could be no separate States in Islam but only regions which were at times in revolt against the Caliph; this theory was retained even when the Arab Empire had disintegrated and there were independent Arab kingdoms in Spain, North Africa, Egypt, and Mesopotamia. The jurist ignored these happenings so that they never worked out a system which might, for instance, have included Arab Nation-States. The world was viewed as one State composed of Muslims, with non-Muslim subjects allowed to carry on their religions under certain conditions, and non-Muslim countries; with these there could be no 'diplomatic' relations, for the Muslim world was considered to be either at war with them, or in a state of truce. There seemed no reason to begin to evolve any form of international law to meet the changing conditions.

INDEPENDENCE UNDER IBN TULUN

When Ahmed ibn Tulun was sent from Baghdad in AD 868 as Governor to Egypt, and there set himself up as an independent ruler, he was regarded as a rebel against the Caliph of Baghdad. In the nineteenth century when the concept of nationalism had been imported from the West, some Egyptians looked back on the Tulunid period as the beginning of a separate Egyptian identity in Arab times. Ibn Tulun, the son of a slave and trained as a professional soldier, was an intelligent and cultivated man who had studied Muslim theology and the Traditions in the University of Tarsus in Anatolia. Owing to the discovery of treasure, probably from ancient Egyptian tombs, he was able to build a new suburb, a palace with nine gates, and his beautiful mosque which remains one of the glories of Cairo, simple, elegant, and majestic, influenced certainly by the architecture of Samarra in Mesopotamia.[36] The Tulunid dynasty lasted until AD 933.

FATIMID CALIPH IN CAIRO

The Abbasids from Baghdad had never exerted much control over North Africa, and in the tenth century there were three Caliphs – an Ummayyad Caliph of Spain, a Shia Fatimid Caliph in Tunis centred on Qairawan, and the Sunni Caliph at Baghdad. In AD 969 the fourth Fatimid Caliph, al-Muizz, sent his general, Jawhar, a Mameluke of European origin, to invade Egypt. He defeated the Ikshid governors, who had followed the Tulunid dynasty, and prepared a palace for the reception of the Caliph; to house his troops a new town was built to the north of al-Fustat and called al-Kahira ('the victorious'). Jawhar also laid the foundation of the great Mosque of al-Azhar in April AD 970, and it was completed three years later when the Caliph al-Muizz entered the city and took up his residence in the palace which had been built. During the subsequent two centuries of its life additions were made and the palace is said to have contained as many as four thousand rooms. Al-Fustat remained the main centre of commerce; ships brought goods from the East and tied up at extensive wharves, for the Nile then flowed about half a mile farther to the east than it does today; but the seat of government was in and around the Caliph's palace in al-Kahira or Cairo.

In AD 988 the Mosque of al-Azhar was made into a university and became the most famous in the Muslim world. While Alexandria had become an insignificant city by the end of the ninth century with a population which had fallen from about six hundred thousand to one hundred thousand, all the wealth of the new rulers was lavished on al-Kahira and al-Fustat. The Fatimids loved elegant decorations on stucco generally in arabesque; but they also portrayed the human figure. This was disapproved of in Mecca and Baghdad since Muslims considered that it might lead to a return to idolatry. The Persian traveller, Nasir-i-Khrusran, wrote in the eleventh century that the Mosque of al-Amr at al-Fustat, although less elegant than the newer Fatimid mosques, was still considered as the most important one. He described the houses as being seven storeys high and containing as many as three hundred and fifty people and there were two hundred inns, or *khans*; the markets were full of roses, lilies, narcissi, and fruit and there were wonderful days of festival when thousands of people came to enjoy themselves at al-Fustat.[37] As Europe began to grow in prosperity from the eleventh century there was an increased demand for spices, incense, silks, and other com-modities from the East and Egypt gained considerable wealth from this trade. Some of Alexandria's past glories returned through trade with the Venetian Republic.

THE CHRISTIAN CRUSADES

Under the first Fatimid Caliph al-Muizz and his son al-Aziz, who was married to a Christian wife, the rule was tolerant, but there followed the mad al-Hakim, who persecuted the Christians and destroyed many churches including, in AD 1010, the Church of the Holy Sepulchre in Jerusalem. This was one of the causes of the Christian Crusades which lasted from the end of the eleventh century to the end of the thirteenth century. The first Crusaders from Europe found the Muslims divided; at the end of the tenth century the Seljuk Turks, who were Sunni Muslims, had migrated eastwards and captured Baghdad in AD 1055. By the time the Crusaders reached Syria the Seljuk Empire had broken up into a series of small States and the Caliph of Baghdad ceased to have much power.

By the end of the eleventh century the Fatimids had lost part of Syria to the Seljuk Turks and the rest to the Christian Crusaders. In 1168 King Amalric advanced from Jerusalem and threatened al-Fustat but al-Kahira was saved by an order from the Fatimid Vizier that al-Fustat should be burned and the fire raged for over fifty days.

SALADIN, SON OF AYYUB

In AD 1171 Salah a-Din Yusuf ibn Ayyub, the Kurd (known as Saladin), presided at the death of the last of the Fatimid Caliphs and set up his own family dynasty of Ayyubids with only very nominal allegiance to the weakly Caliph of Baghdad. There was now once more religious unity under the Sunni faith while Egypt and Syria were brought together again under the rule of Saladin. He pre-vented the Crusaders under Richard I of England, 'the lion-heart', from capturing Jerusalem and he kept them out of Egypt.

Saladin was the most outstanding figure taking part in the Crusades, following the precepts of the first Caliph that a covenant made must be kept, whereas the Christian Bishops told the Crusaders that they need not keep faith with the Saracens since they were infidels. To Sir Walter Scott, writing his *Talisman* in 1830, it seemed a 'singular contrast' that Saladin should have been a better man than Richard I; yet the Saracens were heirs to a civilization over four centuries old and, in comparison, the Crusaders were 'barbarians', who had to wait nearly three centuries for their own Renaissance. There were exceptions among the Crusaders, but on the whole the Saracens regarded them much as the Arab geographer, al-Masudi, in the tenth century, had described the men of the North: 'Their bodies are large, their natures gross, their manners harsh, their understanding dull and their tongues heavy. . . . Their religious beliefs lack solidity. . . . Those of them who are farthest to the north are the most subject to stupidity, grossness and brutishness.'

Saladin made many improvements in Cairo and some have described it as Saladin's city, but there have been many influences; under the Tulunids it was the architecture of Mesopotamian Samarra, under the Fatimids a gayer and more Mediterranean impulse, under the Ayyubids and the Mamelukes architects began to develop their own style, though at first there were Syrian influences and later Turkish from Constantinople. Saladin followed the Syrian custom of having a Saracen castle built to dominate the town and he created the great Citadel up against the Mokhattam Hills overlooking the whole of Cairo. The Ayyubids and the Mamelukes developed the area where the Fatimids had built. The old city of al-Fustat, which was about two miles away from the main town of al-Kahira or Cairo, had been built again after the burning; but by the middle of the thirteenth century it had suffered neglect. Ibn Sa'id al Maghrabi travelling in Egypt from North Africa during the years 1240-9 was depressed by al-Fustat and found the walls of the Mosque of al-Amr scribbled over in charcoal and red paint, but the people were remarkably polite and he never tasted sweeter water than from the River Nile at al-Fustat. But it remained an important centre of commerce: 'As for the merchandise from the sea of Alexandria and the sea of the Hejaz which comes to al-Fustat, it is beyond description; for it is here that it is collected and not at al-Kahira, and from here it is forwarded to all parts of the country; and it is in al-Fustat that we find the sugar and soap factories and most of other such-like establishments'. It was not until the bed of the Nile moved farther westwards, roughly to its present position, that the old city of al-Fustat declined.

The Christian Crusaders continued to look at Egypt with envious eyes, but it was not until the Sixth Crusade at the beginning of the thirteenth century that an attempt was made from Europe to capture the country; having landed at Damietta the Crusaders did not reach farther west than Mansurah where they were defeated and eventually had to withdraw. St Francis of Assisi had visited the Saracen camp alone and obtained good terms but these were refused by the Crusaders. The ninth Crusade was led by Louis IX of France in another attempt to win Egypt, but this had an even more disastrous ending with the capture of the King and the slaughter of many hundreds of knights. Joinville, the historian who accompanied the King, gave a vivid account of the battles and of the murder by the Mamelukes of Touran Shah, the last descendant of Saladin. Ahmad al-Bedawi, of Tanta, who died in AD 1276 and became the local saint, played an important part in working up the population against the Christian Crusaders.

The Muslims who had been tolerant to Christians before the Crusades became less tolerant and there was a legacy of hostility and mutual ignorance. The Christians were considered by the Muslims to be idolaters believing in a Trinity of three Gods, while the Christians believed the strangest stories of the Muslims. Europe was to benefit from what the Crusaders had learned of Muslim fortress-building, architecture, learning, and poetry, but for the Muslims of the eighth to thirteenth centuries there was little for them to learn from Europe even if they had wished to look for it. 'Philosophy is the special province of the unbelievers: we have it all from them', wrote Roger Bacon in the thirteenth century.[38]

BAIBARS SAVES EGYPT
The Mameluke Turk Baibars became Sultan of Egypt after the end

of the Ayyubid dynasty; once again, as Saladin had done, uniting Egypt with Syria. He saved this area from the devastation of the Mongol hordes which had crossed the River Oxus and entered Persia under Ghengis Khan of Mongolia. After his death, Prince Hulugu advanced to the destruction of Iraq and Baghdad which ended the rule of the Abbasid Caliphate in Baghdad. But Baibars made the wise move of setting up a member of the Abbasid family in Cairo as Caliph, though the power remained in the hands of the Mameluke Sultans. When the Ottoman Turks conquered Egypt in 1517 they took the Caliph back with them to Constantinople; from then the Ottoman Sultans claimed that they inherited not only the political power held by the successors of the Prophet Mohammed but also the spiritual power. Egypt and Syria remained moderately prosperous, as compared to Iraq which did not recover until the twentieth century from the breakdown of civilian government and the destruction of the network of irrigation canals.

Much of the wealth of the Arabs came from the monopoly of trade they had enjoyed between East and West across Mesopotamia to the Gulf, across Arabia through Petra in Jordan to Aqaba, and across Egypt to the Red Sea, Aden and India; but much of this trade was deflected to Europeans when the Portuguese in the early sixteenth century had established themselves on the west coast of India, having opened up a trading route round the Cape of Good Hope. 'The Arab Near East had been outflanked. Not until the nineteenth century did the life-giving flow of world trade return', states Professor Bernard Lewis in his *Arabs in History*. There were, he writes, three significant events; firstly, the Islamic Near East was changed from a commercial monetary economy to a feudal economy based on agriculture; secondly, it was the end of the political inde-pendence of the sedentary Arabs and of the Arabic-speaking peoples who were replaced by the Turks; thirdly, the centre of gravity of the Arabic-speaking world shifted from Iraq to Egypt – 'with the power of the Arabs went the glory'. Syria and Egypt continued as the main centres of Arabic culture but 'passive dependence on authority in public life found its parallel in literature'.

By the end of the sixteenth century much of the trade in the ports of the eastern Mediterranean was increasingly handled by the French and English, who were granted certain privileges by the Ottoman Sultans, known as 'Capitulations'. These gave them the protection of their own consuls and was to become a system from which the Muslims suffered serious abuse. 'It was at first not a concession wrung from a weak Oriental Power, but the granting, by a gesture of almost condescension, of the rights of *Dhimmis* in Muslim society, extended by the inner logic to foreign Christians.'[39]

The Muslims knew very little of Europe even then and had heard only dimly that there had been some kind of renaissance; they continued to believe that they were still the most civilized, the most wealthy, and the most religious people in the world. Even the much-travelled Ibn Khaldun, 'that outstanding genius who attempted in the fourteenth century to construct afresh a scientific foundation for history',[40] was only vaguely aware that there were changes in Europe and wrote: 'We have heard of late that in the lands of the Franks, that is, the country of Rome and its dependencies on the northern shore of the Mediterranean, the philosophic sciences flourish. . . . But God knows best what goes on in those parts.'

4   European interest in Egypt

A GREAT DEAL had been going on in Europe with the Renaissance of the fourteenth to sixteenth centuries, but little attention was
paid to Egypt or the countries of the Middle East until Elizabethan
times. The Crusades had created a hostility between Muslim and
Christian which has not perhaps even yet been entirely eradicated; the
creation of Israel, for instance, reminded Arabs of the trouble that
they had had over the Christian Crusaders and they recall that in the
end the foreigners had to leave.

The travellers who came to Egypt from Elizabethan times onwards found not only hostility but also a people depressed in spirit
and in their economic life. Terrible famines in the eleventh and
thirteenth centuries led to cannibalism in Cairo; the later Mameluke
rulers exploited the Fellaheen and the traders, and the Ottoman
Turks, after conquering Egypt in 1517, took the best Egyptian
artisans to work in Constantinople. 'Ottoman power, which was
not sufficient to preserve order within Egypt, was, however, great
enough to shield it from European infiltration, and the country spent
the next three centuries in a stupor, unaware of the vast revolutions
that were taking place across the Mediterranean and by-passed by the
Renaissance and the Industrial Revolution.'[41]

It was only the European students of Arabic who could appreciate
the people, understand their background of civilization, and give
Europe a fair picture of what the Egyptians were like. But the other
travellers, who were the majority, could only describe that they found
a disorderly and unhappy people.

64

'In my opinion', wrote James Capper in a book published in 1783, 'they are now . . . the most disagreeable and contemptible nation on the earth, bearing no relation to the former Egyptians'; Mr H. Rooke in a book published in the same year referred to the Egyptians' 'languid and effeminate spirit' and their 'lack of courage to resist tyranny', and Professor J. White wrote: 'Where shall we find a degeneracy like that of the present race of Egyptians, or where an ancient inheritance of greatness and glory, which had been so totally wasted and lost'.[42] They did not understand the religion of Islam and believed that it was responsible for the state of the country and would die as a religion. Even the knowledgeable Carsten Niebuhr, who was in Egypt from 1761 to 1763, wrote that the Egyptians had always been known 'as a melancholy and obstinate people overridden with superstition'.

ANCIENT EGYPTIAN MONUMENTS

Most of the travellers concentrated on visiting the ancient Egyptian monuments of Upper Egypt, many of which were half buried in sand. They were described and drawn by Richard Pococke (1704–65), later Bishop of Meath; also by Frederic Nordin (1708–42) of the Danish Navy who made the first survey of the country; Étienne Fourmont (1683–1745), the French Orientalist, James Bruce of Kinnaird (1730–94), and others.

The accounts and drawings they brought back to Europe aroused great interest. Between them they had visited nearly all the most important monuments of ancient Egypt except for those which were distant from the Nile. Brought up in a Graeco-Roman tradition they preferred the later Ptolemaic and Roman buildings to the more remarkable monuments of the early Egyptian dynasties. Even the drawings they made of these earlier monuments lost much of their Egyptian character and tended to become Hellenic in style. 'Vision was falsified by education, academic tradition, memories of the Renaissance and the habits of thought in western Europe under Louis XIV and Queen Anne.'[43] But interest was stimulated and as soon as these books were published in one language they were translated into others.

ISLAMIC ARCHITECTURE

Hardly any of these travellers mentioned the remarkable Islamic architecture of Cairo. Only the Frenchman Benoît de Maillot (1656–1738), who went to Cairo in 1692 as French Consul and stayed there for sixteen years, wrote of such buildings as the Mosque of Sultan Hasan, of al-Azhar, and of al-Amr. 'What is most curious about the mosques', he wrote, 'are the domes and minarets. One cannot sufficiently admire the beauty of these domes, their grace, proportion, boldness and above all the astonishing grandeur of some. The ornamentation and decoration inside is no less worthy of consideration.'

Although the Crusaders had learned much from the art of the Saracens in the building of fortresses and from the elegance of their palaces and mosques and almost sub-consciously imported new ideas which affected European architecture and poetry, it was another two centuries or so before the European traveller began to realize that there was beauty in the art of the 'infidel'. It should be added, however, that it was very difficult for the foreign visitor to enter the mosques, so strong was the feeling of hostility against the Christian Frank; the mosques were often hidden by high walls or enclosed by little streets, and it is only when inside that it is possible to realize their full beauty.

The seventeenth and eighteenth centuries were periods of great turmoil in Egypt, when Mameluke factions were fighting one another or in revolt against their suzerain, the Sultan of the Ottoman Empire. 'There is not on earth', wrote James Bruce, 'a more brutal, unjust, tyrannical, oppressive and avaricious set of miscreants than are the members of the government of Cairo.' The haughty airs of the proud Scottish nobleman, which enabled him to be on good terms with the wild Ethiopian leaders, served no useful purpose in Cairo. 'Before the French invasion', wrote William Hamilton about conditions in 1801, 'no Frank or European traveller was permitted, except by special favour, to mount horses in Cairo. In general they were reduced to go on foot, or to make use of asses, when they paid their visits or went in search of curiosities. When we were there, this distinction had been for sometime laid aside, and Europeans thus

mounted were not afraid even of meeting a Bey or a Turk; a pre-
sumption which a few years ago would have been attended by some
unpleasant consequences.'[44]

DEFENCE OF MUSLIMS: W. G. BROWNE

The first to question the prevailing Christian belief that the Egyptians
could not make progress because they were Muslims and 'infidels'
was W. G. Browne. He came to Egypt in 1792 following in the
footsteps of James Bruce whom he much admired. He did not think,
however, that the discovery of the Blue Nile had answered the whole
question and came to look for the source of the White Nile, but was
held up in Darfur. In his book[45] he had an interesting chapter
entitled 'Comparative View of Life and Happiness in the East and
in Europe' which led a reviewer to accuse Browne of being an
'infidel' and prejudiced against Christianity. Browne considered that
the backwardness of the Egyptians was due to their lives under
foreign invaders; it was not due to any inferiority in themselves or
their religion. He pointed out that the Muslims had the same view
of crime as other nations; their Arabian and Persian histories and
romances contained stories of magnanimity, generosity, justice, and
courage which were in no way inferior to those of other nations
and sometimes set a higher standard. 'The Greeks and ourselves', he
wrote, 'have indeed stigmatized them with the name of barbarians,
but impartial enquiry pronounces that they are susceptible of all that
is admired in a polished people.' He agreed that fatalism might
prevent Muslims taking steps to avoid evils, but it gave them
dignity and stopped them repining; 'the European, attributing more
power to volition, ascribes to his own want of judgement or energy
the result of whatever terminates unfavourably. Thus a part of his
life is occupied by self-accusation which, however, ensures no
amelioration for the future.'

SAVARY AND VOLNEY

Another sympathetic visitor was Claude-Étienne Savary (1750–88),
an Arabic scholar who stayed in Egypt for three years (1776–9),
translated the Koran, and wrote a life of Mohammed. His book,

Lettres sur l'Egypte, was published in 1787 and was at once translated into English passing quickly into three editions. C./F. Volney (later a Baron), also a Frenchman, published a book in the same year, which also had a great success and was immediately translated into English; he wrote intelligently of Egypt but he did not like it and thought that Savary was much too enthusiastic. He had decided to travel as the best method of 'adorning the mind and forming the judgment' and he prepared himself physically and mentally: 'not-withstanding all our efforts', he wrote, 'our judgments are much less directed by the real merits of objects, than by the impressions we receive, or carry with us in viewing . . . to see well is an art which requires more practice than is commonly imagined'. But he did not always manage to rid himself of his European viewpoint:

> It is with reason, therefore, that the Egyptians have always pro-fessed, and still retain, a religious veneration for the Nile; but an European must be pardoned, if, on hearing them boast its beauty, he smiles at their ignorance. Never will these troubled and muddy waters have for him the charm of transparent fountains and limpid streams; never, except for some extraordinary excitement, will a swarthy Egyptian woman, dripping from these yellow and muddy waters, remind him of the bathing Naiads.[46]

He considered that it was essential to know Arabic 'to appreciate either the language or the genius of a nation'; but after eight months in Egypt he was disillusioned and went to learn Arabic in Syria where he stayed for two years.

These books by Savary and Volney were informative and well written but there was another and stronger reason why they were so widely read in England, France, and Europe. Interest had been aroused in Egypt because it was on the route to India, much of which had been taken over by the East India Company following the victories of Clive in the middle of the eighteenth century. There was still rivalry between Britain and France, who had fought the Seven Years War (1756–63). During the French Revolution Robespierre's dictum was 'perish the colonies rather than our principles', but it was not very long before Talleyrand and Bonaparte were urging the advantage to be gained from colonies especially in West Africa and Egypt and in July 1797 Talleyrand became Foreign Minister.

BONAPARTE INVADES EGYPT

Volney was strongly opposed to the annexation of Egypt and published a pamphlet in 1788, *Considerations on the War with the Turks*, stating, 'the characters of both nations [French and Egyptian] being diametrically opposite in every respect, would become mutually odious'. Bonaparte, however, believed he could win over the Egyptians by 'liberating' them from the Mamelukes. When he landed with his army and captured Alexandria in July 1798, he proclaimed, 'I have come to restore to you your rights and to punish the usurpers. I worship God more than the Mamelukes do, and I respect his Prophet Mohammed and the admirable Koran . . . tell the people that the French are also true Muslims.' With Bonaparte came the famous Commission on the Sciences and Arts consisting of one hundred and sixtyseven scientists, mathematicians, Orientalists, naturalists, engineers, artists, irrigation experts, Arabists, and an Arabic printing press. Bonaparte intended to find out as much as possible about Egypt and exploit its capabilities as a colony. At the same time he and his civilian planners were full of Revolutionary zeal to help the oppressed Egyptians, and they expected them to welcome French aid in throwing off the rule of the 'alien' Mamelukes. Bonaparte was full of friendliness towards the Shaikhs of alAzhar and other notables and he wanted them to think that he and his army were quite prepared to become Muslims and be, as it were, part of the Egyptian community; but they would need just one or two dispensations, being allowed, for instance, to drink wine and to remain uncircumcised. The Shaikhs refused to accept such liberties.

The entertaining contemporary Egyptian historian, Shaikh Abd alRahman alDjabarti,[47] made it clear in his long account that the Egyptians were not taken in by the French, nor did the Shaikhs like their ways nor their Revolutionary ideas – it was just another invasion, this time by infidels, and sooner or later the French would

69

go. When Bonaparte released his Mameluke prisoners after the Battle of the Pyramids many of them, poverty-stricken, took refuge in the Mosque of al-Azhar. 'They fed', wrote Shaikh al-Djabarti, 'on the alms distributed to them by the poor students'; the oppressors when in need were helped by the oppressed, 'in this those who have eyes to see will observe a beautiful example'. In spite of the misery which had been caused by Mameluke rivalries, Egyptians accepted the situation passively for their oppressors, Mameluke or Turk, were Muslims and subjects of the Sultan of Turkey and they had been taught for centuries to be obedient to their rulers. They did not regard the Muslim Mamelukes as foreigners, though many were Circassians from the Caucasus, but the French were regarded as foreigners because they were infidels.

Egyptians belonged to a closely knit, complex Islamic society within the Ottoman Empire kept together by the religion of Islam which engendered a feeling of brotherhood for everyone who was a Muslim from whatever country he came. Neither the French, nor other foreign visitors, understood that ideas of territorial or ethnic nationalism were entirely alien to Muslims, nor were they interested in French proposals of reform for these, too, were all alien. But some were impressed by the amount of learning which was displayed in the French Institute which was open to all, including its large library of Arabic books. Shaikh al-Djabarti, who was himself well known as a mathematician, expressed his admiration for the French enthusiasm for learning; he used to visit the library and attend lectures on electricity and chemistry. The fact that the French of the Revolution were not Christians made them appear less suspect and led some of the young Egyptian writers and teachers to study their ideas on liberty and nationalism; slowly some of these ideas began to exert an influence.

From the point of view of Europe the remarkable achievement of the French expedition was the amount of well-documented material brought together describing every aspect of Egypt – its land, waters, people, trades, animals, fish, birds, reptiles, and ancient monuments. This was eventually published in the great work in ten huge volumes of text and fourteen volumes of plates, called *Déscription de l'Egypte*.

VIVANT DENON

One of the remarkable members of the French Commission was the charming and attractive Dominique Vivant Denon, later to become a Baron and Director of the Beaux Arts in Paris. He went into Upper Egypt with the French troops under General Desaix, pursuing the remnants of the Mameluke forces which had rallied after the Battle of the Pyramids. Denon was as good at writing as he was at drawing. His book, published in 1802, was immediately popular in both French and English.[48] Of the Pyramids of Giza he wrote: 'The great distance from which they can be perceived makes them appear diaphanous, tinted with the bluish tone of the sky, and restores to them the perfection and purity of the angles which the centuries have marred.' 'The expression of the face is gentle, graceful and serene', he wrote of the Sphinx. 'The mouth, with its thick lips, has a sensuality in its sweep and a refinement of execution that are truly admirable.'

Denon was fifty years of age when he went on this exhausting and dangerous expedition to Upper Egypt – 'scarcely had we described an antiquity than we were forced to leave it' – but he writes with an enthusiasm as if he were in his twenties. 'I was traversing a country which Europe scarcely knows except by name', and he was worried lest the Mameluke leader, Murad Bey, would surrender so that the French Army would no longer advance and enable him to draw the monuments. The army reached Aswan after travelling two hundred and fifty miles in ten days. 'Pencil in hand I passed from object to object, drawn away from one thing by the interest of another.... I had not eyes or hands enough, my head was too small to see, draw and classify everything that struck me. I felt ashamed at the inadequacy of the drawings I made of such sublime things.' Although Denon had been brought up to think that Greek architecture of the best period was the standard of beauty, he realized that he was confronted with something quite different. 'One must avoid the common error', he wrote, 'of thinking that Egyptian architecture represents that art in its cradle; on the contrary one must say that it is its standard.... Having borrowed nothing from other nations, the Egyptians added not one extraneous ornament, not a single superfluity to the lines dictated by necessity.'

Nothing bored Denon except copying the hieroglyphs, 'minute details of dull pictures, stripped of sense'. It was not long, however, before French surveyors, irrigation experts, and others were madly copying hieroglyphs because a discovery had been made at Rosetta. At a meeting of the French Institute in Cairo on 19 July 1799, the members had been greatly elated by a message received from a fellow-member, announcing 'the discovery at Rosetta of some inscriptions that may offer much interest'. Indeed, this was the famous Rosetta Stone, now in the British Museum, which contained on a block of basalt a trilingual inscription written in Greek, in hieroglyphs, and in what Herodotus had called 'demotic', the cursive form of ancient Egyptian writing. It was realized, that here, perhaps, was the key to the ancient Egyptian language of hieroglyphs. The Greek inscription was nearly complete and could be read; it was a decree issued by the Egyptian priesthoods honouring Ptolemy V in 196 BC, and it seemed very likely that the other two inscriptions were a repetition, but it was over twenty years before hieroglyphs could be deciphered.

FRENCH EVACUATION

With the destruction of most of the French fleet by Nelson in Abukir Bay, the return of Bonaparte to France, and the assassination of General Kleber in Cairo, most of the French officers and men were eager to leave Egypt. The British landed at Abukir Bay on 8 March 1801, and a battle was fought at Canopus with very heavy casualties on both sides, especially on the French. 'I never saw a field so strewed with dead', wrote Sir John Moore in his diary. The British Commander-in-Chief, General Sir Ralph Abercrombie, died of his wounds and General Hutchison took over. By July the French had capitulated in Cairo and by August in Alexandria.

With the British forces was William Hamilton, sent on a diplomatic mission by Lord Elgin who was Ambassador in Constantinople; he was asked by General Hutchison to ensure that the Egyptian monuments were handed over in accordance with the terms of the surrender; the French had, in fact, already taken the most precious objects on board a hospital ship in the harbour. Hamilton, with an escort of British troops, managed to extract a sarcophagus, which was incorrectly considered to have been that of Alexander the Great, and the Rosetta Stone, both now in the British Museum.

WILLIAM HAMILTON

Hamilton then left for Cairo and Upper Egypt and wrote in his *Ægyptica* the best account of the country at that time. He gave a good description of the view from the Citadel of Cairo which is similar to the view today, except for the addition of a number of sky-scrapers.

> The citadel commands the whole town. . . . The view from the hall of the castle to the south and west is one of the most striking in Egypt. It extends from the pyramids of Giza to those of Memphis [Saqqara] and Dashur, at the foot of which appears to flow the venerable Nile; the range of mountains to the east, ending in the quarries and abrupt precipices of the Mokhattams, enclosing as it were Old Cairo, its mosques, and tombs of the Mameluke Sultans in the desert space immediately below.

He described the ceremony of cutting the canal bank, which brought water from the Nile into the city; this happened about the middle of August 'when it is known by the *mekkias* (nilometer) that the Nile has risen to the height of sixteen cubits, the public crier having proclaimed the gradual rise of the flood every day since the inundation had begun'. He considered that the Ezbekieh Square, or *Midan*, with its fine houses was the handsomest part of Cairo in spite of the terrible destruction following the revolt in Cairo against the French. With the cutting of the canal bank 'the centre of this square is filled with water, and the traffic across it is carried on by boats. . . . At night frequent parties of pleasure with bands of music are to be seen in different parts of the lake. In the dry season this amusement gives place to that of practising, during the cool of the day, the *djerêd* exercise on horseback. Some of the houses in and about Cairo have very large gardens, laid out with considerable taste. They are all abundantly supplied with Nile water, have summer houses or kiosks, where the thick palms or sycamores afford them shade.' 'Those who are overwhelmed with want of occupation,' wrote the French traveller Sonnini, 'and this is the lot of the rich, repair to the gardens, and, always seated, they delight in breathing a fresh and balsamic air, or in listening to bad music.'[49]

Hamilton estimated the city of Cairo to be about eight miles in circumference and surrounded on all sides by a high stone wall. In spite of the confusion and the poverty following the French evacuation, he made a shrewd prophecy, 'Egypt is likely to become within a few years a very interesting subject of discussion in Europe. It will no longer be considered as merely an object of curiosity to the antiquary; the dismemberment of the Turkish Empire, should it take place, will bring Egypt, with several other eastern provinces, into the sphere of European politics.'

At the time that Hamilton was in Egypt no leader had emerged. Mohammed Ali the Albanian, who had come to Egypt with the Turkish force to fight the French, was still manœuvring to achieve power, exploiting first the Mamelukes and then the Turks, but in 1805 he was elected ruler by the Shaikhs and notables. In 1811 he finally broke the power of the unruly Mamelukes by inviting their leaders to a banquet at the Citadel and then having them massacred. 'A soldier who assisted at the massacre', wrote Dr Madden, 'informed me that the poor wretches, in their despair, kept running to and fro, from one door to another, vainly seeking a place of safety, until there was not a single Mameluke left standing. . . . The soldier said that it was lamentable to see such fine clothes as they wore spoiled with blood.'[50] This could have been the Italian Giovanni Finati, originally conscripted into the French Army, he had enlisted under Mohammed Ali and had become a Muslim. It is interesting to note the way that English and French soldiers, who had been taken prisoner, were accepted into the Egyptian community once they had agreed to become Muslims. When the Vicomte de Chateaubriand arrived in Cairo in October 1806, there were about one hundred French soldiers who had deserted from the army and decided to remain in Egypt as Muslims. Chateaubriand wrote that they had, like Alexander the Great, adopted the customs of the country, 'they wear long silk robes, fine white turbans, superb arms; they have a hareem, slaves, horses of the best breed, all the things that their fathers had not got in Gascony and Picardy'. Burckhardt's servant, Osman, who had accompanied him on his travels in Arabia, had been a soldier with General Frazer's ill-fated expedition to Egypt in 1807, defeated by Mohammed Ali's troops. Kinglake wrote that Osman suffered captivity, conversion and circumcision, passing through the fire of Mohammed Ali's Arabian Campaigns, but 'they could not cut away or burn out Osman's inborn love of all that was Scotch'.

THE AFRICAN EXPLORERS: J. L. BURCKHARDT

A new type of traveller to Egypt arrived following the formation of the African Association in London in 1788 under the Presidency of Sir Joseph Banks. As a result of the deaths of Mungo Park and a number of other explorers to West Africa who had been trying to discover the course of the River Niger, it had been decided that a better approach would be to accompany one of the Muslim caravans which crossed the Sahara westwards from places such as Cairo. With this object in view the African Association sent out the young Swiss, John Lewis Burckhardt. After he had spent two years in Syria learning Arabic he went to Egypt and in February 1873 reached Aswan, 'the most romantic spot in Egypt'. He had acquired a great interest in the Arabs and liked their proverbs which he considered showed with what wisdom they judged of men and things. 'The natives in general are so fond of figurative language and of witty allusions and comparisons taken from low life, that these sayings are constantly quoted on every common occasion, and express the tendency or moral of an event much better than would be done by a long and flowery speech.'[51] Burckhardt travelled as far as the Second Cataract near the Egyptian boundary north of Wadi Halfa, and found the four colossal statues at Abu Simbel almost buried by sand, 'the entire head and part of the breasts and arms of one of the statues are yet above the surface'; there was little to be seen of the next one and of the other two 'the bonnets only appear'.[52]

Burckhardt was very much concerned about the slave-trade out of Africa and estimated that there were at least forty thousand slaves in Egypt, of whom two-thirds were male and the rest female, and during the plague of the spring of 1815 in Egypt eight thousand were reported to have died in Cairo alone. 'There is hardly a village in which several of them are not found, and every person of property keeps at least one.' Captain Henry Light, on leave from military duty in Malta, was offered in Assiut in 1814 'a young well-formed Negress, about seventeen years old, for the trifling sum of rather more than fifteen pounds sterling'.[53] Thomas Legh, MP, had found prices even lower the year before: 'girls whose virginity was secured by means more powerful than moral restraint were valued at 500 piastres – female slaves who could not boast of this advantage were in general sold for 300 piastres'.[54]

Burckhardt praised the laudable efforts made in Europe, especially by England, to stop the slave-trade, but added that even that would not abolish slavery in Africa; the Atlantic slave-trade was 'trifling compared with the slavery of the interior'.

As long as those countries [such as the Sudan] are possessed by Mussulmans, whose religion induces them to make war upon the idolatrous Negroes, whose domestic wants require a constant supply of servants and shepherds, and who, considering slaves as a medium of exchange in lieu of money, are as eager to obtain them as other nations might be to explore the African mines, slavery must continue to exist in the heart of Africa; nor can it cease until the Negroes shall become possessed of the means of repelling attacks and resisting the oppression of their Mussulman neighbours.

Burckhardt argued that Europe must carry out a wise and grand plan leading to the civilization of the continent and he recommended 'the education of the sons of Africa in their own country, and by their own countrymen, previously educated by Europeans'. It was a long-sighted view taken by this kindly, courageous, and knowledgeable Swiss; at the same time he had faint hope that anything would be done by European governments 'for the remote and despised Negroes, while selfishness and a mistaken policy have prevented them from attending to the instruction of their own poor'. He wrote thankfully that the practice of turning slave boys into eunuchs was dying out, though there was still at that time a village near Assiut where the chief 'operators' were two Coptic monks; in the autumn of 1813 sixty boys were emasculated there and two of them died, which was considered a small percentage.

The Nubians lived in the valley, where the Nile is kept to a narrow channel between sandstone hills and only fertilizes a small strip of land on either bank; they emigrated to Cairo and the Delta for work, as they have always done. 'They generally act as porters (*bowabs*)', wrote Burckhardt, 'and are preferred to the Egyptians on account of their honesty.' After staying for eight or ten years they returned to their land and resumed their simple life. The Nubians, or Berbers, have a passion for their own country, poor as it is; the new High Dam built under the régime of President Gamal Abdel Nasser floods their former homes so that the Egyptian and Sudanese governments have been faced by the difficult and tragic problem of moving one hundred thousand Nubians from their homeland to another area.

THE SCRAMBLE FOR ANTIQUITIES: BELZONI AND DROVETTI

After his remarkable journeys as a Syrian merchant to Nubia and Mecca, Burckhardt returned to Cairo, known to his Arab friends as Shaikh Ibrahim Ibn Abdullah, and made friends with a small group consisting of Henry Salt, the British Consul-General, who had made his name by his travels in Abyssinia, William Turner,[55] a young diplomat, and the Italian giant, Giovanni Belzoni, who had acquired fame in the circuses of England but was now looking for new fields to conquer. They often met at the hospital table of Boghos Bey, the Armenian adviser to Mohammed Ali, who had been very nearly thrown into the Nile in a sack when he failed to find the money the Pasha demanded. They were all interested in ancient Egyptian antiquities and Burckhardt roused Belzoni's enthusiasm by describing the buried giants of Abu Simbel. They talked of the huge granite head of 'young Memnon' (Ramesses II), which lay near Thebes, a mass of stone weighing nearly eight tons. It had been described by William Hamilton as 'the most beautiful and perfect piece of Egyptian sculpture', and Bernard Drovetti's gangs

77

had tried to take it but it had proved too heavy. Drovetti, the French Consul, had fought in Europe in Napoleon's army, and was an eager collector of antiquities with numerous agents working for him in Upper Egypt. Henry Salt was also an enthusiast and had been encouraged by Sir Joseph Banks and others to collect for the British Museum.

Burckhardt and Salt decided to try to obtain the giant 'Memnon' head for the British Museum, making use of Belzoni's ingenuity. 'He handles masses of this kind', wrote Burckhardt to London, 'with as much facility as others handle pebbles, and the Egyptians who see him a giant in figure, for he is six feet and a half in height, believe him to be a sorcerer.' Belzoni was delighted at the plan and travelled at once to Thebes, which made a deep impression on him. 'It appeared to me like entering a city of giants who, after a long conflict, were all destroyed leaving the ruins of their temples as the only proofs of their former existence'.[56]

There was bitter national rivalry over antiquities between Salt and Drovetti, who had to work out spheres of influence over the tomb areas in order to avoid gang battles. It was ironic, therefore, that the British Museum refused one of Salt's large consignments of antiquities, which he sold to the Louvre, while the French government would not buy Drovetti's collection; this was sold to the King of Sardinia and helped to form the Museum of Egyptology in Turin. The French clergy had argued strongly against the purchase 'on the grounds', writes Stanley Mayes, 'that the study of Egyptian antiquities would destroy fundamentalist belief in the Bible; in particular it was thought that Egyptian history might upset the established view as to the date of man's first appearance on the earth'.

LIVING WITH MUMMIES

In the early nineteenth century Mohammed Ali, who had gained control of the whole of Egypt and was planning various military adventures abroad, saw no objection to giving Europeans permission to look for ancient Egyptian tombs. Permission to dig or to use Arab labour depended, however, very largely on which of the interested parties gave the largest bribe to the local official. Many of the Fellaheen near Thebes and Luxor lived in the tombs at places like Gourna (Qrna) and worked as labourers to remove large monuments or sold mummies to wealthy visitors. 'The staple commodity of Gourna consists in mummies', wrote Dr Madden; 'the Arabs find it easier to live by selling dead men than by the toil of husbandry'. They also sold 'mummy powder' mixed with butter as a medicine which was supposed to cure internal and external ulcers. This had been done for centuries; as early as 1586 John Sanderson, a member of the Levant Company, visited Egypt and shipped to England for the London apothecaries five hundred-weight of mummy fragments.

Dr Madden in the account of his travels described visiting one of the Arab troglodytes of Gourna:

His dwelling was in the most spacious chamber of a superb sepulchre, the walls were covered with ancient paintings, the roof was supported by four magnificent pillars, his divan was formed of an inverted coffin, and the lamp, which feebly illumined this gloomy chamber, was made of the cover of an alabaster vase; various antique utensils furnished his cupboard, and the screen which separated the women's alcove from the common chamber, was formed principally of the linen torn from the mummies.

Madden explored farther along the tunnels leading into the cliff face and was followed by four little troglodytes, the eldest being about eight years old; 'and now in the chamber where the dreariness of the scene and the sickening sight of these cadaverous mummies made me shudder, they sat on the broken coffins, pulling about the rigid arms of the dead bodies, and playing with the gilded fingers of a mummy which had been dragged from the coffin'. Belzoni, too, had some strange stories to tell; the tomb-dwellers would invite him to dinner of chicken 'baked on a small oven heated with pieces of mummy cases, and sometimes with the bones and rags of the mummies themselves'.

There had certainly been great destruction of Egyptian antiquities through the centuries, and it was only the coming of the Europeans that made the Muslim authorities gradually realize how valuable and interesting were these ancient remains. In the scramble for these antiquities some of the Europeans caused damage but they saved a great deal more than they destroyed.

THE EGYPTOLOGISTS

In the first half of the nineteenth century the secrets of the ancient Egyptians began to be revealed by the discovery of the key to the decipherment of hieroglyphs. Twenty years had passed since the discovery of the Rosetta Stone and there was still uncertainty. Akerblad, a Swedish diplomat, had started to decipher the demotic inscription which he realized was the writing referred to by Herodotus, and he found that it bore a resemblance to the existing Coptic language; he believed it was an alphabet and not mere symbols. The talented and versatile Englishman, Thomas Young, had by 1814 completed the translation of the demotic inscription and was on his way to some understanding of the less complete hieroglyphic text; in 1823 he published his results (*Account of the recent Discoveries in Hieroglyphic Literature and Egyptian Antiquities*). The race was on, as it was to be a little later with the decipherment of cuneiform. The Englishman, Henry Rawlinson, won the cuneiform race and the Frenchman, Jean-François Champollion, was the first to exploit his success in deciphering hieroglyphs.

CHAMPOLLION

Champollion worked on a copy of the texts from the Rosetta Stone, and on inscriptions from the Cleopatra Obelisk which Belzoni had sent from Philae to the home of William Bankes at Kingston Lacy in Dorset; he also received copies of inscriptions and drawings of cartouches on Nubian temples from Frederic Cailliard, a mineralo-gist in the service of the Pasha, who travelled south of the Second Cataract to Meroe and Fazoogli with a military expedition sent by Mohammed Ali in 1820. On 29 September 1822, Champollion made his historic announcement on decipherment to the Paris Academy in the form of his *Lettre à M. Dacier* — Secretary to the Academy. In 1824 he published *Précis du Système hieroglyphique* in which he revealed that he had deciphered the names of Ramesses and Thutmosis among others.

There was much dispute about his findings, but he was confident and officially supported. In 1828 two missions left Europe for Egypt, one led by Champollion and financed by the French government, the other led by the Orientalist Rosellini and financed by the Duke of Tuscany. Drovetti had tried his utmost to prevent the missions from leaving. Salt had died in 1826 and Drovetti had expected to have the monopoly in collecting Egyptian antiquities, but now there would be rivals, and Government control; the authorities of Paris and Turin would, wrote Drovetti, 'gâter le métier'. In his many letters to the authorities he exploited the fact that Mohammed Ali Pasha was furious and in no mood to grant permission to antiquity-hunters, for in 1827 English, French, and Russian ships had sunk the Egyptian and Turkish fleets at Navarino.

When Champollion arrived in Egypt Mohammed Ali had calmed down, and permission was eventually given for him to visit Upper Egypt. On 16 November 1828, he was able to read by the light of lanterns and of the moon on the walls of the Temple of Denderah (Tentyrah) the names in hieroglyphs of Roman emperors such as Tiberius, Claudius, and Nero. Most of the temple did not date earlier than 100 BC and had received high praise from travellers; by moonlight it had appeared impressive to Champollion, but when he saw it in stark sunlight next day he declared the sculptures to be in the worst styles, 'the bas-reliefs are detestable and that is not surprising; they belong to a decadent period'.[57] He showed his good taste by emphasizing the importance of Beni Hassan and of Deir el-Bahri for the history of architecture. When Champollion arrived at Wadi Halfa on New Year's Day, 1829, he wrote to M. Dacier to say that the alphabet needed no modification, it could decipher the inscriptions of the Pharaonic periods as well as of the Roman. He began to bring out the great work *Les Monuments de l'Egypte et de la Nubia* but died of apoplexy at the age of forty-two and his disciples published the rest of the series.

GARDINER WILKINSON

Funds were now being raised by various European countries to send out missions and the people who came were scholars and

Egyptologists, able to devote all their time to making a proper survey of the monuments. Drovetti was right in realizing that the great days of the traffic in antiquities were over, though there was still money to be made in supplying the private collector. John Gardiner Wilkinson took to the study of Egyptology after leaving Oxford and made it his profession; he published *The Topography of Thebes and General Survey of Egypt* in 1835 and his well-known book *Manners and Customs of the Ancient Egyptians* was published in three volumes in 1837, fully illustrated with delightful engravings. We find the theories of Herodotus still being much discussed, but now an Egyptologist, such as Gardiner Wilkinson, knew, in many respects, more than Herodotus, even though he had spoken with ancient Egyptians.

RICHARD LEPSIUS

Another scholar who took up Egyptology as a career soon after the death of Champollion was the German, Richard Lepsius (1810–84), who visited a number of the collections of ancient Egyptian antiquities which by this time had been made in London, Paris, Turin, Florence, Bologna, and Leyden among other places. Financed by the King of Prussia, he headed a mission which arrived in Egypt in 1842. In their serious German way the members of the mission spent Christmas Eve in the burial chamber of the Great Pyramid and sang the Prussian National Anthem, while Lepsius lit the candles on a palm tree planted in the sarcophagus and surrounded by Christmas presents.

For three years they explored the Egyptian and Ethiopian monuments from south of Khartum to the coast of Syria, and in 1859 the results were published in twelve large volumes. In 1866 Lepsius returned to Egypt and discovered the important Decree of Tanis, or Table of Canopus, which was a trilingual inscription like the Rosetta Stone; he later published a grammar of the little-known Nubian language. Many scholars in England, France, and Germany were working on hieroglyphic texts as more and more of them were copied. 'The rivulet of Egyptological research', writes Sir Alan Gardiner, 'was gradually swelling into the mighty stream which now makes it impossible for any student to keep abreast of all that is written save at the cost of abandoning all hope of personal contributions.'

THE COPTIC LANGUAGE

Champollion had been helped in his decipherment of hieroglyphs by his knowledge of the Coptic language. In 1807, at the age of sixteen, he read a paper before the Grenoble Academy in which he maintained that it was the language of ancient Egypt. Coptic spelling did, in fact, give an idea of the pronunciation of ancient Egyptian – there were four main Coptic dialects – but from the tenth century the Copts mostly wrote in Arabic; it was still spoken in Upper Egypt as late as the fifteenth century but soon afterwards became a dead language. Sonnini, who visited the monasteries in the Wadi Natrun about 1782, wrote that the services were conducted in Arabic or Greek Coptic but that the old Coptic language was unknown to them and nor did they understand the Greek or modern Coptic, although some of the prayers were repeated in that form. He described the monks as 'anticipating death by a useless and savage life, making it their sole study to counteract the laws of nature and, having abjured the quality of men, endeavouring to form a barren colony for heaven'. He found them ugly, filthy, and disgusting. 'Poor fellows', wrote Robert Curzon, 'they meant well, and knew no better; and what more can be said for the endeavours of the best of men.'

Robert Curzon, who arrived in Egypt in 1833, was one of a number of keen seekers after Coptic manuscripts and wrote a delight-ful book which became a classic.[58] Besides the monasteries of Wadi Natrun he visited those in Upper Egypt built in the desert, or on the top of high rocks such as 'the Convent of the Pulley'. Most of them were built like fortresses and inside he found the architecture very interesting: 'After the remains of the private houses of the Romans at Pompeii, they are the most ancient specimens extant of domestic architecture. . . . The monastery of St Catherine at Mount Sinai has hardly been altered since the sixth century and still contains orna-ments presented to it by the Emperor Justinian.' He visited the ancient Egyptian temples and tombs which had for many centuries been taken over as Christian churches and commented:

> The inner court of the Temple of Medinet Habu has also been converted into a Christian Church; and the worthy Copts have daubed over the beautifully executed pictures of Ramesses II with a coat of plaster, upon which they have painted the grim figures of hermits, whose uncouth forms would almost give one the idea of their having served for a system of idolatry much less refined than the worship of the ancient gods of the heathen, whose places they have usurped in these gigantic temples.

The travelling Dr Madden gave an interesting account of the trans-formation made by the early Christians of the ancient Egyptian gods. The statue of Osiris had been altered to a representation of the Christian Divinity; the figures of Isis with the child Horus in her arms were made personifications of the Virgin Mary and of the Christ child; Typhon answered for the Devil with the addition of a tail and hooves, and a procession of Egyptian priests had become a company of Apostles.[59]

The Coptic churches in what was the old Fort of Babylon in Cairo and the various monasteries in different parts of Egypt are still well worth visiting today. Lady Russell in her excellent book wrote of Wadi Natrun: 'These monasteries have a history of nearly sixteen hundred years and are still living entities today . . . in them we have a survival of the early Middle Ages, preserved as in amber before our eyes.'[60]

'THE ARABIAN NIGHTS'

So far the European travellers, except for Herodotus, had been interested mainly in antiquities, Coptic manuscripts, conquest, and to a certain extent medieval Arab buildings, but the Egyptian people are scarcely mentioned. A book, however, had appeared at the beginning of the eighteenth century which excited great interest; it gradually became famous and revealed to Europeans that the Arabs, which included the Egyptians, were not after all as gloomy, dull, and uncivilized as they had thought, but were a jovial, witty people who enjoyed erotic, adventurous, and magical stories. This was *The*

Thousand and One Nights published in French in twelve volumes (1704–17) by the Orientalist Antoine Galland. Later there were other translations of the work from the Arabic, including one by Edward Lane.

Lane had already published in 1836 his delightful and informative book *Manners and Customs of the Modern Egyptians*, which remains perhaps the best book on Egypt even today; though some of the customs he describes have disappeared, many are still to be found if looked for. He revealed, as Burckhardt had done in a small way, the great variety, humour, and vitality of Egyptian life. 'The Egyptians', he wrote, 'are particularly prone to satire, and often display considerable wit in their jeers and jests. Their language affords them great facilities for punning, and for ambiguous conversation.' Lane considered that if the English reader possessed a close translation of *The Thousand and One Nights* with ample notes, he could have spared himself the trouble of writing his first book, for it presented 'most admirable pictures of the manners and customs of the Arabs, and particularly those of the Egyptians'; the most extravagant of the stories were not regarded, even by the educated classes, as incredible.

> I have resided in a land where genii are still firmly believed to obey the summons of the magician or the owner of a talisman, and to act in occurrences of every day; and I have listened to stories of their deeds related as facts by persons of the highest respectability, and by some who would not condescend to read *The Thousand and One Nights*, merely because they are fictions, and not written in the usual polished style of literary compositions.[61]

Eventually Lane made a translation of this remarkable work with extensive notes, for he considered that it was representative of life in Egypt as he knew it: 'it is in Arabian countries, especially in Egypt, that we see the people, the dresses and the buildings, which it describes in almost every case, even when the scene is laid in Persia, in India or in China'. There was some criticism that Lane had exaggerated. The stories were certainly Persian and Indian, as well as Arab, in origin and were referred to in the tenth century by al-Masudi in his book called *The Golden Meadows*, but Lane considered

that they had been rewritten in Egypt. Certainly an Arabic collection of tales called *The Thousand and One Nights* had existed in Cairo
in the twelfth or thirteenth century, describing the background of
life during the Mameluke period.

By the nineteenth century the book had become famous throughout Europe. 'That wonderful work,' wrote Richard Burton, 'so often
translated, so much turned over, and so little understood at home.
The most familiar of books in England, next to the Bible, it is one
of the least known, the reason being that about one-fifth is utterly
unfit for translation, and the most sanguine Orientalist would not
dare to render literally more than three-quarters of the remainder.'[62]
But he published privately a very full translation thirty years later and
the Victorians of England were so eager to buy copies that he made
sixteen thousand guineas. Burton was critical of Lane for omitting
'objectionable' words and passages.

ORIENTAL VIEWS ON SEX

The Oriental has always treated sex very much more openly than the
Victorians. 'The most immodest freedom of conversation', wrote
Lane, 'is indulged in by persons of both sexes, and of every station of
life, in Egypt, even by the most virtuous and respectable women . . .
things are named, and subjects talked of, by the most genteel women,
without any idea of their being indecorous, in the hearing of men,
that many prostitutes in our country would abstain from mention-
ing.' Lane, Browne, and Robert Curzon considered that the evils
of the hareem system had been much exaggerated by some writers.
Curzon pointed out that the Christian women lived from choice in
the same way as the Muslim women and the veil acted as a disguise
which gave them a greater freedom than women in Europe; Curzon
had several times been addressed by Turkish and Egyptian ladies in
the open street 'and asked all sorts of questions in a way that could
not be done in any European country'.

LUCIE DUFF GORDON

Europeans often found that things Egyptian did not turn out quite
as they expected. Gerard de Nerval, the French Romantic, bought

in the slave market near the Mosque of al-Azhar a beautiful girl from Java called Zeynab, the heroine of his *Voyage en Orient*; she was not prepared to cook or do any work and he had to increase his household to have her looked after, so that he became more of a slave to her than she to him. 'There are a good many things about hareem here which I am barbarian enough to think extremely good and rational', was the comment of Lady Duff Gordon, who lived for seven years in Egypt trying to recover from consumption, and wrote a series of shrewd and observant letters to her family in England.[63] She lived for many years as the only European in Luxor in a house built by the English Consul-General Salt when Belzoni and he were obtaining antiquities. It was perched on top of the pharaonic columns of the Temple of Khem and from there she observed life on the Nile and in the village. She wrote the best account of what was going on in the country-side in the 1860s under the Khedive Ismail who ruled Egypt from 1863 to 1879; she had wisdom, tolerance, and some interesting comments on the English.

The English would be a little surprised at Arab judgments of them. They admit our veracity and honesty and like us on the whole, but they blame the men for their conduct to women. They are shocked at the way that Englishmen talk about hareem among themselves, and think the English hard and unkind to their wives and to women in general. . . . The fundamental idea in it all, in the mind of an upright man, is, that if a man 'takes up' with a woman at all, he must make himself responsible for her before the world; and above all things for the fate of any child that he may have had by her.

What she wrote is true of 'the upright man', but divorce is easy; the ratio of divorces to marriages has been thirty per cent during recent years.

Lucie liked the social equality which was to be found in Cairo and the country districts:

As in *The Thousand and One Nights*, great Beys sit with grocers, and carpenters have no hesitation in offering hospitality to *naas omra* (noble people). This is what makes Arab society quite unintelligible and impossible to most Europeans. . . . As there is no education and no reason why the donkey boy who runs behind me may not become a great man, and as all Muslims are *ipso facto* equal, money and rank are looked on as mere accidents, and my *savoir faire* was highly thought of because I sat down with Fella-heen and treated everyone as they treat each other. In Alexandria all that is changed. The European ideas and customs have extinguished the Arab altogether and those who remain are not improved by the contact.

Lucie became interested not only in the lives of the country people but also in their beliefs.

Egypt is a palimpsest, in which the Bible is written over Herodotus and the Koran over that. . . . The sacred animals have all taken service with Muslim saints. . . . Maree Girgis (St George) is simply Amen ra, the God of the Sun and the great serpent slayer, who is still revered in Egypt by all sects, and Sayyed al-Bedawi is as certainly one form of Osiris. His festivals, held twice a year at Tantah, still display the 'objectionable' symbol of the creator of all things. All is thus here. The women wail the dead as on their old sculptures . . . directly contrary to the Koran; the observances at birth and the almost worship of the Nile, which are not Muslim but ancient Egyptian, these are a few of the ancient things and in domestic life are numbers more.

At Keneh she was invited to an Arab party where there were danc-ing-girls, but she found their dancing cold and uninteresting. Then the Captain of the *dahabieh* called out to a woman named Latifeh, 'an ugly clumsy-looking wench', to show what she could do.

And then it was revealed to me. The ugly girl started on her feet and became the 'Serpent of Old Nile'. The head, shoulders and arms eagerly bent forward, waist in and haunches advanced on the bent knees – the posture of a cobra about to spring. I could not call it 'voluptuous' any more than Racine's *Phèdre*; – it is: *'Venus toute entière a sa proie attachée'*, and to me seemed tragic. It is far more realistic than the fandango and far less coquettish, because the thing represented is *au grand serieux*, not travestied or played with, and like such things the Arab men don't think it the least improper! . . . She moved her breasts by some extraordinary muscular effort, first one and then the other. They were just like pomegranates and gloriously independent of stays or any support.

Lucie criticized the English visitors for being taken in by the lavish expenditure of the Khedive Ismail to impress them with the 'progress and civilization', and for not studying the effects on the country people who made up the wealth of Egypt. She did not like a book published by her cousin, Harriet Martineau, which was full of statistics with little mention of the Egyptians.

The people are not real people, only part of the scenery to her, as to most Europeans. She evidently had the feeling of most English people here that the difference of manners are a sort of impassable gulf, the truth being that their feelings and passions are just like our own. . . . It is curious that all the old books of travels I have read mention the natives of strange countries in a far more natural tone and with far more attempt to discriminate than modern ones, e.g. Niebuhr's travels here and in Arabia, Cook's Voyages and many others. Have we grown so *very* civilized since a hundred years that outlandish people seem like mere puppets, and not real human beings to us ?

Each traveller saw the kaleidoscope of Egyptian life very differently. Kinglake stated 'there is not much in the way of public buildings to admire at Cairo', a remark which would have earned the contempt of Mr Creswell.[64] Eliot Warburton had disliked 'the filthy, intricate lanes and alleys' of Cairo, while Lucie Duff Gordon found them delightful and the people so friendly 'they give hospitality with their faces'. Several writers expressed their dislike and contempt for the Arabs, while Dr Madden wrote, 'the more I see of the Arabs, the more I am convinced they are naturally the kindest hearted people in the world'. Gerard de Nerval wrote to a friend that he could not think of Cairo, that 'City of a Thousand and One Nights', without remembering all the things he disliked: the English in their elegant carriages, the Turks dressed like Europeans, the foreigners like Orientals, and the new palaces built like barracks. Thackeray expressed his pleasure at seeing 'England in Egypt . . . with their pluck, manliness, enterprise, bitter ale and Harvey sauce', while Pierre Loti vehemently expressed his dislike of the Anglo-Saxon tourists on their Nile-boats – 'snobs and imbeciles'. 'It is curious to see the travellers' gay *dahabiehs* [Nile-boats] just as usual', wrote Lucie Duff Gordon in 1865 during a year of especial hardship, 'and the Europeans as far removed from all care or knowledge of these distresses as if they were at home. When I go and sit with the English I feel almost as if they were foreigners to me too, so completely am I now *Bint el Balad* (daughter of the country) . . . and thus out of "my inward consciousness" (as Germans say) many of the peculiar-ities and faults of the people are explained to me and accounted for.'

Many argued that the introduction by Mohammed Ali and his successors of steam-boats, railways, new palaces, the opening up of old streets, and the building of the Suez Canal were signs of pro-gress; the Khedive Ismail, who said that he wished to make Egypt part of Europe, had many supporters until he brought bankruptcy to Egypt. Lucie Duff Gordon's daughter, Janet, was married to Henry Ross, a Director of Briggs's Bank in Egypt and involved in many of the plans for development, but Lucie saw things differently: 'I care less about opening up trade with the Sudan and all the new railways – and I should like to see person and property safe, which is not the case (Europeans, of course, excepted). . . . What is wanted here is hands to till the ground.' She pointed out that the Fellaheen were taken away on the hated *corvée* to build the Suez Canal, or 'hideous barrack-like so-called palaces'. 'What chokes me', she wrote, 'is to hear the English people talk of the stick being the only way to manage Arabs, as if anyone would doubt that it is the *easiest* way to manage any people where it can be used with impunity.' The Khedive Ismail had persuaded the Sultan of Turkey to let him have ninety thousand *feddans* (one feddan being a little more than an acre) of uncultivated land as his private property; he then exchanged this for land which had been cultivated. It belonged to Turks who had been given land eight years previously by the Viceroy Said Pasha, who had the sensible idea of founding a landed aristocracy. The Turks for eight years spent their capital in cultivation and then were forced to sign a contract handing it over to the Khedive Ismail 'or they go off to Fazoogli – a hot Siberia whence none return'.

In January 1865, Lucie Duff Gordon wrote:

> Last week the people were cursing Ismail in the streets of Aswan, and everyone talks aloud of what they think. The whole place is in desolation. . . . The courbash has been going on my neighbours' backs and feet all the morning. It is a new sensation, too, when a friend turns up his sleeve and shows the mark of the wooden handcuffs and the gall of the chain on his throat! The system of wholesale extortion and spoliation has reached a point beyond which it would be difficult to go. . . . One's pity becomes a perfect passion, when one sits among the people, as I do, and sees it all; least of all can I forgive those among Europeans and Christians who can help to 'break these bruised reeds'.

Two years later she wrote:

> When I remember the lovely smiling landscape which I first beheld from my windows, swarming with beasts and men, and look at the dreary waste now, I feel 'the foot of the Turk' heavy indeed. Where there were fifty donkeys there is but one. Camels, horses are all gone; not only the horned cattle, even the dogs are decimated, and the hawks and vultures seem to be fewer; mankind has no food to spare for hangerson.

It is not surprising that the Khedive Ismail sent threatening messages to her and tried to have her turned out of the country, for her letters were being published in England from 1865 onwards and went into several editions. Her testimony is important for she was the only English person settled in the countryside, who described what was happening. It was a critical period; the vast expenditure by Ismail on showpieces led to bankruptcy, his own deposition, and the British occupation of Egypt.

18 During the Ptolemic Dynasty (323–30 BC) Alexandria became the capital of Egypt. An engraving of Alexandria showing one of Cleopatra's obelisks in the foreground.

19 (*right*) The spread of Christianity started from Alexandria in *c.* AD 45. An eighteenth-century drawing of the monastery of St Paul near Thebes.

20 After the conquest of Egypt by the Arabs in the seventh century the capital was first Al Fustat and later Al Kahira (Cairo). An eighteenth-century engraving of Cairo from the Saladin's citadel.

21 The beautiful lithographs of David Roberts made in the early nineteenth century reveal much of the life of the period at Cairo.

22 The monastery of St Catherine at Sinai was built by the Emperor Justinian in the sixth century AD.

23 The Arab ruler Ahmed Ibn Tulun built his great mosque in AD 876–9. This is the courtyard with the ablution fountains on the left and the Minaret in the background.

24 (*left above*) Bonaparte, when he invaded Egypt in 1788, did his best to ingratiate the Shaikhs of al-Ahzar. He is seen here unbearded in Muslim costume.

25 (*left below*) Murad Bey, one of the Mameluke leaders of Egypt, who was defeated by the French at the Battle of the Pyramids in 1798.

26 (*above*) At the 'Battle of the Nile' Nelson defeated the French fleet and Bonaparte's army was isolated in Egypt. A nineteenth-century engraving showing the French flagship exploding.

27 Bernard Drovetti and his men collected antiquities for France. His main rival was the British Consul, Henry Salt.

28 (*left*) John Lewis Burckhardt (1784–1817), Swiss explorer and orientalist.

29 (*right*) Giovanni Battista Belzoni (1778–1823), the Italian 'giant', famous for his archaeological discoveries, in Oriental dress.

30 *The Thousand and One Nights* (*The Arabian Nights*), when published, revealed magical, witty and erotic stories about Eastern life. This engraving is from the later English version of 1865 by Edward Lane.

31 One of the Cairo houses illustrated in the French publication of *Description de l'Egypte*, compiled by Bonaparte's 'scientists' in the eighteenth century.

32 (*above*) A Turkish bath house in the eighteenth century; one of the many aspects of Egyptian life revealed in *Description de l'Egypte*.

33 and 34 (*below, left and right*) Methods of irrigation – always a problem for the Egyptian.

5   Europe's impact

'The impact of the West was indeed a hurricane force and the Muslims were unprepared for it.' GAMAL ADBEL NASSER, *Philosophy of the Revolution.*

BEFORE THE INVASION OF EGYPT by Bonaparte, the Muslims of western Asia, of Africa, and of Arabia had been secure from Europe for three and a half centuries behind the shield of the Ottoman Empire. Indeed, it seemed in the seventeenth century as if the Muslim Turks, having conquered southern Europe, would engulf the north too, as the Arab Muslims would have done in the eighth century if it had not been for the successful resistance of Christian Constantinople in AD 718; or again, if it had not been for Charles Martel's victory at Poitiers in 732, 'perhaps the interpretation of the Koran would now be taught in the schools of Oxford, and her pulpits might demonstrate to a circumcised people the sanctity and the truth of the revelation of Mahomet'.[65]

The Turks, however, had twice failed to seize Vienna and at the end of the eighteenth century the Russians had taken from them the whole of the Crimea peninsula. They knew that the Europeans had acquired superior military strength and skill, but the Egyptians in their isolation had not understood the changed circumstances, and the warlike Mamelukes were amazed when the French Army invaded and conquered Egypt so easily. Two illusions had been shattered, one that Muslims were safe from Europeans, and the other that Muslims were civilized while Europeans were barbarians. Egyptians began to look at Europeans with great interest, for it was essential to find out why they had become so powerful as to be in a

The Ottoman Empire in the seventeenth century; the areas in Asia and Africa became eleven independent states in the present century.

position to control much of the world. There was even danger that they might conquer the whole Ottoman Empire, unless their secret could be discovered.

Mohammed Ali, when he became ruler of Egypt, decided to introduce European institutions and learning. He founded his own form of State control of the land, built factories to try to industrialize the country, and formed his own army. He began to lose interest, however, when England, under Lord Palmerston, prevented his army's advance to the destruction of the Ottoman Empire and when his manufactured goods could no longer be protected, following the Anglo-Turkish Convention of 1838, which allowed Europeans to trade freely anywhere in the Ottoman Empire.

The historian al-Djabarti strongly objected to the autocratic powers assumed by the Viceroy Mohammed Ali Pasha: 'if God had given him a little justice along with his determination . . . he would indeed have been the wonder of his age, and the peace of his time'.

It has been argued that al-Djabarti was right to oppose Mohammed Ali's progressiveness, for it lead to 'the dissolution of all the values of Islamic civilization'.

Islam is a 'religion' and a 'social' order at one and the same time. You cannot upset the social order without harming the religion and endangering the whole structure of the Islamic world. . . . Egyptian intellectuals of later generations have pushed aside al-Djabarti's objections. They followed the West, its ideas and arrangements blindly without ever wanting or being able to give up their old civilization entirely. Where that will lead to no one can foretell with certainty; but it often seems as if they are unable to escape from the circle of 'tyranny' which began with Mohammed Ali and which al-Djabarti resisted in vain.[66]

Those who are favourable to Mohammed Ali's reforms, and call him the maker of modern Egypt, consider that contact between Europe and the Muslim world had been too long delayed already and further postponement would have made the impact all the more devastating. Once the full power and influence of Europe hit the Middle East the effect was far-reaching. Muslims realized that they could not survive unless they adapted themselves quickly. That was extremely difficult; they received the full impact of the Industrial Revolution without having had time to adjust themselves to the ideas of the European Renaissance. Muslims had to borrow alien institutions and ideas ready-made without having the time necessary to modify them to suit their own history, way of thinking, and manner of life. The religion of Islam had brought them up to think on quite different lines to the European and it was under strong attack as being responsible for their backwardness.

SPECIAL POSITION OF ISLAM

There is tension in all religions in such circumstances. That was shown in the disputes regarding Christianity in Alexandria during the third and fourth centuries; and again when the Muslims also had been influenced by the Greek philosophers during the eighth and ninth centuries; that had led to conflict between reason and revelation, and between the transcendence of God and the doctrine of immanence; or, to jump many centuries, when the Christian Church felt itself assailed by the Darwinian theory of natural selection during the nineteenth century. But there was a further complication; Islam also embraced the laws governing civil life. Whereas Jesus Christ lived under the Roman Empire and had no need to draw up a civil code for his followers – 'render unto Caesar the things that are Caesar's' – the Prophet Mohammed had to form a government from a community of merchants and Bedouin; laws and customs were established which, with the teaching of the Traditions after Mohammed's death, became known as the *Sharia*. Islam therefore regulated not only the relations between man and God but between man and man and man and woman; all was divinely inspired, according to orthodox Muslims, and therefore could not be tampered with. Under a Christian government it was possible to separate the moral laws taught by the Church from the practical laws of the State; if they conflicted there was seldom a serious social or psychological crisis, but Islam was interpreted by the orthodox in such a way as to allow no separation. 'The decisive moment in the history of Muslim civilization' was the moment when the orthodox theologians 'rejected the conceptions based on Greek logic, which were later to exercise a determining influence on Western civilization'.[67]

Most of the orthodox Muslims continued to ignore Europe, but there were some, even in the early days, who considered that it was essential to explore Europe's secrets of power.

SEARCH FOR THE TALISMAN

Some of the problems facing the Muslims are revealed in the explorations of Europe in the first half of the nineteenth century. The first educational mission sent to Paris in 1826 by Mohammed Ali was headed by Rifa'ah Rafi al-Tahtawi (1801–73) who had been at the University of al-Azhar for ten years first as student and then as teacher; he was a man of great energy and enthusiasm, and was delighted by Paris, except for the liberty allowed to women which made it 'the Paradise for women but Hell for men'. The French

Orientalists in Paris were interested in his learning and in exchange they helped him to acquire French; he read Voltaire, Racine, Montes-quieu, Rousseau, Greek philosophy, and the history of ancient civilizations; he studied mathematics, geography, and physics. He was surprised to find that the French were wealthier, better educated, and more intelligent than Egyptians and yet they were not Muslim. It was an extraordinary experience and the book he wrote (al-Takhlis al-ibriz) – the first book on Europe to be given to the modern Arab world – was immediately very widely read. This was followed by a second book (al-Manahij) in which he described how to develop as a nation.

He pointed out that in ancient times Greece and Egypt exchanged knowledge with profit to both, and argued that the Muslim *Ulama* (doctors of law) and theologians should make themselves aware of such things as 'natural law' and the learning of Europe, rather than avoiding all contact with ideas outside those of Islam; otherwise how could they interpret the Sharia in the light of modern needs. Al-Tahtawi pointed out that the sciences spreading in Europe had been handed on from the Greeks by Islamic writers and there was no harm in taking back what had once belonged to Islam.[68]

In this second book – 'the greatest single influence on the thought of Egypt in the nineteenth century'[69] – al-Tahtawi set out what was meant by citizenship, describing the rights, duties, and code of behaviour for rulers, for the Ulama and judiciary, for soldiers, and for peasants and craftsmen. This was an entirely new concept, as was the principle of patriotism which he described; he wrote a history of Egypt from Pharaonic times to the Arab Conquest and saw no reason why the glories of ancient Egypt should not be regained. There was certainly opposition to al-Tahtawi's ideas from many of the Ulama of al-Azhar, but he was a loyal subject and had the support of Mohammed Ali.

One of the men he influenced was the Tunisian, Khayr al-Din Pasha, who published a book in Arabic in 1867, which was later translated into French as *Réformes nécessaires aux États musulmans*, and aroused great interest. He became Grand Vizier to Sultan Abdul Hamid but failed to persuade him to carry out the reforms which he considered necessary. He criticized the orthodox Muslim view 'that all acts and institutions of those who are not Muslims should be avoided', and argued that the learning of Europe should be studied; its strength lay in 'political institutions based on justice and freedom'. Defending himself against the Muslim traditionalists he wrote that in taking such things from Europe they would not be taking anything from Christianity; it was not Christianity which was responsible for progress, otherwise the Papal State would be the most advanced in Europe instead of the most backward.

In the first flush of their enthusiasm al-Tahtawi and Khayr al-Din saw no reason why it should not be possible for Muslims to become part of the modern world while remaining orthodox in their religion. The dangers had not yet begun to be realized.

RISE OF THE NATIONALISTS

European ideas, however, spread very slowly at first. A Shaikh of al-Azhar, Mohammed Abdu, who was to become famous and exert an influence which is still felt today, considered that 'the people at home got nothing of the fruits of these travels and the advantage of the knowledge that had resulted from them'. Under the grandson of Mohammed Ali, the Khedive Ismail, Egyptians left all their general affairs and often their personal ones to the will of the ruler: 'Although Ismail', wrote Mohammed Abdu, 'set up a Consultative Assembly in 1866 whose task it was supposed to be to convince the people that they had a voice in the affairs of their country, never-theless no one, not even the members of the Consultative Assembly itself, believed that they really possessed those rights. . . . They felt that it was still the absolute will of the ruler which governed their opinions.' Mohammed Abdu wanted to limit the power of the ruler and, like al-Tahtawi, to teach the people that they had duties and rights.

There was ferment in the country because of the extravagances of the Khedive Ismail and because of the ever-growing control by the French and British to safeguard the interests of the European share-holders. In the second year that the Consultative Assembly met, 1867, members showed opposition to the Khedive Ismail by emphasizing that they had the right to review the finances; when this caused concern in Europe and a British and a French representa/ tive were appointed to the Cabinet, opposition became stronger.

AL/AFGHANI

'In 1871 there came to our country a remarkable man', wrote Shaikh Abdu, 'with deep insight into religious things, wise in the political affairs of States, full of information and knowledge and with an overflowing heart; this was Sayyed Jamal al/Din al/Afghani.'[70]

The arrival of this slight, bearded, magnetic personality attracted an audience wherever he went; he was one of the most significant figures of modern Islam and helped to inspire what became a revolt, not only against the dynasty of Mohammed Ali but also against France and Britain. Al/Afghani considered that there was no time to be lost for the reform of Islam, for this was the only way Muslims could withstand the onslaught of Europe. In his travels in India, Persia, Afghanistan, and the Ottoman Empire he had found the British, Russians, or French in an increasingly powerful position. He saw everywhere the menace of Europe, as Gamal Abdel Nasser today sees the menace of imperialism. Al/Afghani argued that Muslims allowed themselves to be oppressed because they had the mistaken belief that the British were superior; the British had, it was true, application and determination, which Muslims could also acquire; but he did not believe that they were particularly intelligent.

Both al/Afghani and Mohammed Abdu considered that the *Ummah* or Community of Believers, should be the basic political unit; this was at variance with those who had borrowed the idea of territorial nationalism from Europe. In a different form this remains the problem today in the Arab world.

During his seven years in Egypt, al/Afghani lived near al/Azhar University and lectured to students, journalists, Ulama, Shaikhs, officials, and others. 'Thus', wrote Mohammed Abdu, 'everywhere feelings were aroused, minds stirred and the veil of indifference became thinner in all parts of the country but especially in Cairo. All this was going on while the great Monarch was sitting on his high throne, too high for such radiations to weaken his position.'

Among al-Afghani's disciples were many who were to take the lead in the battle for independence, such as Saad Zaghlul and, of course, Mohammed Abdu himself. The students at al-Azhar had been accustomed to hearing only religious disputation – the Muslim equivalent to the interest St Thomas Aquinas is alleged to have had in how many angels could stand on the point of a needle. Al-Afghani's teaching was largely political and based on his own experience or on what he had learned from history. He drew attention to Guizot's lectures on European civilization, which had been translated into Arabic in 1877, for he liked the will to progress preached by the former French Prime Minister; al-Afghani often quoted the verse of the Koran, 'God changes not what is in a people, until they change what is in themselves' (Sura XIII, 10). These were new ideas and they were received with enthusiasm by his many students.

THE KHEDIVE ISMAIL

In spite of the unpopularity of the Khedive Ismail because of his close association with foreigners and his extravagances, he carried out many important reforms which were of great benefit to Egypt during his reign of twelve years. Money was spent on education, telegraphs, railways, lighthouses, harbours, and irrigation canals; the population increased by one million to five million. 'Egypt is a marvellous instance of progress', wrote *The Times* on 6 January 1876. 'She has advanced as much in seventy years as other countries have in five hundred.' Ismail showed great courage in signing international conventions for the abolition of the slave-trade down the Nile from Central Africa and across to the Red Sea, which was extremely profitable to Egypt; it is estimated that about fifty thousand slaves were sent along these routes annually. There was a tremendous boom in cotton when American supplies to Lancashire were cut off as a result of the Civil War, and Lancashire became dependent on Egyptian exports which increased by four times in value, but then came a recession. Many projects had to be abandoned owing to the ending of the boom, to the mishandling of the finances, and to the crooked dealings of many of the European and local Levantine creditors, who expected exorbitant rates of interest. Ismail was a hard worker and had good ideas for reform but unfortunately considered that he could outwit those who were trying to outwit him. He had revived the system of State trading introduced by Mohammed Ali and he owned about one-fifth of the fertile land of Egypt. In extracting the money that he needed it was always the Fellaheen cultivators who suffered and they grew to hate him, but especially they hated the foreign Christian, Jewish, Copt, and Levantine bankers and usurers into whose hands the Khedive had fallen. He entertained in a style which recalled *The Arabian Nights*.

The Suez Canal, which was opened with a fantastic and expensive festival in 1869 in the presence of the Empress Eugénie, should have been of great profit to Egypt. 'I want the Canal to belong to Egypt, not Egypt to the Canal,' said Ismail; but his wish was not fulfilled. In 1875 he sold the Egyptian shares which were taken up by Disraeli and later he sold his right to fifteen per cent of the profits. Egypt lost not only a great deal of revenue from tourists who no longer used the overland route from Alexandria up the Nile and across the desert from Cairo to Suez, but the profits of the Canal went to others. Until 1937 Egypt received nothing and then was granted three hundred thousand pounds a year. Ismail spent large sums of money as bribes to his suzerain, the Sultan of Turkey, to establish his position and to ensure that his son, Tawfik, succeeded him. It was more money wasted, for the Sultan deposed Ismail in 1879 as a result of pressure from France and England, and it would have been better if Prince Halim Pasha, the able son of Mohammed Ali, had succeeded instead of the weak Tawfik.

TAWFIK AND ARABI

As a result of the distress, the national movement was growing through separate groups often with different aims. There were secret societies and Masonic lodges in which al-Afghani, until his banishment in 1879, and Prince Halim Pasha held important positions; there were the members of the Assembly, enlightened Azharites, and there were many literary periodicals and newspapers; these played an important part as a result of the arrival of a number of able Christian journalists who disliked the restrictions of the Turkish censorship in Syria, and they were helped by the liberalism of Shaikh Mohammed Abdu who was in charge of censorship. The most powerful group was that of the Fellah officers of the army led by Ahmed Arabi who helped to form the National Party in 1879. There were various incidents between the army and the Khedive in which Arabi's popularity with the army was made clear and the Khedive had to give way; Arabi was made Minister of War.

Ahmed Arabi was a peasant born in a Delta village and had risen rapidly to being a Lieutenant-Colonel, during the rule of Said Pasha, who favoured promotion of Egyptians rather than of Turks and Circassians, but after the ruler's death all promotion of Fellah officers stopped. Arabi was a national hero to the peasants who described him as 'The Only One' (al-Wahid). His friend Wilfrid Scawen Blunt described him as tall, heavy-limbed, and slow in movement – 'he seemed to symbolize that massive bodily strength which is so characteristic of the laborious peasant of the Lower Nile'.[71] Arabi, who had studied at al-Azhar where he had met Mohammed Abdu, had read little besides the Koran and a life of Napoleon, but he had shrewd common sense, personal magnetism, and he was a fine orator. He was, however, not a good military commander. His reputation suffered not only as a result of the belittling accounts in the British Press at the time, but also as a result of criticism from other Egyptians, but he is better treated today by President Nasser and others who regard him as the first military leader to fight for Egyptian nationalism. He had great courage in coming forward as leader at that time for there was every reason to think, as he did, that he would be assassinated by orders of the untrustworthy Khedive or banished to the Sudan. That would have happened under Mohammed Ali or Ismail. But when there was the dramatic confrontation between Arabi and Tawfik in September 1881, and the latter proclaimed in reply to Arabi's demands: 'I am the Khedive of the country and shall do as I please' it was the dying cry of a line of autocrats. Arabi's reply is remembered today: 'We are not slaves and shall never from this day be inherited.'

It seemed in 1881 under the Khedive Tawfik that a settlement might be reached. The Assembly was recalled, a more liberal government told that it could produce a Constitution and the civilian and military nationalists affirmed that they would act constitutionally. Even the British Controller, Sir Auckland Colvin, accustomed to AngloIndian methods, reported to London: 'The Liberal movement should in no wise be discouraged. Though in its origins antiTurk, it is in itself an Egyptian national movement. . . . Arabi, who spoke with great moderation, calmness and conciliation, is sincere and resolute, but not a practical man.' It was a golden moment for reconciliation and there had been others, but France and Britain acted otherwise. The movement 'was in its essence a genuine revolt against misgovernment', Cromer was to write later, and of Arabi he said: 'Had he been left alone there cannot be any doubt that he would have been successful. His want of success was due to British interference.'[72]

BRITISH OCCUPATION

Why did Britain interfere? Why did Gladstone, the Liberal Prime Minister, who had encouraged nationalism in Bulgaria and Greece and supported Russia against the Ottoman Sultan, forget his liberalism? He had been sympathetic at first to the national movement of 'Egypt for the Egyptians' which fitted in with the liberal side of his complicated character, even though he and other Liberals were worried that a national movement should be led by military – soldiers should keep out of politics and the memory of the Indian Mutiny was very much alive. They did not realize that the fashion was to give the military the best education and they became the leaders of reform. Wilfrid Scawen Blunt was certainly led astray by the atmosphere favourable to Egyptian nationalists which at first prevailed in England, and was accused later by Egyptian writers of misleading Arabi and other nationalists by his encouragement.

Gladstone retreated from his liberal ideas, probably owing to the disorders and outrages with which he had to deal in Ireland. Two months after the Phoenix Park murders, when the Chief Secretary for Ireland and his UnderSecretary were stabbed to death in Dublin in May 1882, Gladstone had so changed his views that he stated: 'It has been charitably believed, even in this country, that the military party was the popular party, and was struggling for the liberties of Egypt. There is not the smallest rag or shred of evidence to support that contention.'

It was not only Gladstone who was at fault, but also his Foreign Minister, Lord Granville. At the moment when it seemed that all parties in Egypt were beginning to work together Gambetta persuaded Granville to agree to the disastrous Anglo-French Note of 8 January 1882, which showed that the two governments supported the Khedive against the nationalists; that united the civilian and military nationalist leaders; from that moment no one in Egypt was prepared to compromise. The French and British had appeared off Alexandria with their fleets, and the Egyptians had been convinced that another invasion was planned; the French had occupied Tunisia in 1881. There was strong feeling against foreigners throughout the country which broke out into serious rioting in Alexandria and in some of the towns in the Delta. Clashes between Christians and Muslims were reported by the British representatives in Egypt, which caused violent feelings in England and France. It is not surprising that there was rioting and that a number of Christians were killed, considering the threat from the warships and considering that for several years great bitterness had been aroused against the British and French controllers of finance, foreign officials who drew large salaries, and the profit-making Christians and Levantines. Foreigners were sheltered by the Capitulations, which gave them the right to be tried in their own Consular courts and not be subject to Egyptian law if the case concerned foreigners only; if the Egyptian government wished to pass a law which might affect foreigners, it was necessary for agreement to be obtained from a large number of European nations.

The Europeans drew their high salaries and lived in their extra-territorial and tax-exempted communities. The 'Turkish' upper class collected their rents, and were almost as tax-exempt. . . . It all had to be got out of the Fellaheen who were ground to dust. . . .

The Powers had, in fact, themselves created the militarism that they now felt themselves compelled to crush.[73]

The sequel is well known. Alexandria was bombarded by the British Navy in July 1882. Lord Granville thought that that would be sufficient to lead to the fall of Arabi, as Sir Anthony Eden seventy-four years later was to think that a landing at Port Said would lead to the downfall of Nasser. In both cases the prestige of the national leaders was enhanced and their position strengthened. In 1882 fifteen thousand troops were sent from England and five thousand from India under the command of Sir Garnet Wolseley; the Khedive betrayed the nationalist cause and sought refuge with the British Navy; the battles of Kafr-Dawar, Kassassin, and Tell el-Kebir were fought and Arabi defeated; he was tried with Mohammed Abdu and other nationalists; Lord Dufferin came from Constantinople to arrange that the nationalists should be exiled and not run the risk of meeting death at the hands of the Khedive and a vengeful group of Turks and Circassians; the Egyptian Army was dissolved by order of the Khedive, and Evelyn Baring (Lord Cromer) arrived as Consul-General to rule Egypt.

EVELYN BARING (LORD CROMER)

On the death of Gambetta the French government had altered its policy and refused to be drawn into the British adventure, but France did her best to make things difficult for Baring. One of the first things he had to do was to re-create an Egyptian Army to deal with the growing power of the Mahdi in the Sudan. It is possible, as some authors have argued, that, if it had not been for the weakening of the authority of the Egyptian government and of the Sultan of Turkey as a result of British and French action, the Mahdist movement would not have been allowed to assume the formidable proportions that it did. Then there was finance. Besides the already large debt from the time of Ismail there were now additional claims on Egypt, such as the burning of Alexandria, which was probably started by the shells from the British warships, the cost of the Sudan operations, and other claims which amounted to nearly ten million pounds. The European governments were determined that the British should ensure that all the debts were paid. To prevent the confusion of still further foreign control it was necessary to save Egypt from bankruptcy and that Baring achieved.

Baring was handicapped by the fact that successive British governments repeatedly made official statements affirming their intention to leave Egypt; there were forty formal undertakings to withdraw according to a French critic.[74] But plenty of reasons were always found for remaining, such as the defence of India, the need to protect the Suez Canal, and the danger that Russia, having nearly occupied Constantinople in 1878, might force her way into the Mediterranean and threaten the Canal. All the same, Lord Salisbury wrote in February 1887, when Foreign Minister: 'I heartily wished we had never gone into Egypt. . . . But the national or acquisitive feeling has been roused; it has tasted the flesh-pots and cannot let them go.' There was another reason: having once started on reforms, British officials wished to remain to see that they were carried through. Baring's abilities were appreciated by the British govern-ment and he was made a Baron in 1892.

MUSLIM REFORMERS

After his exile from Egypt in 1879 al-Afghani had gone to Paris where he was joined by Mohammed Abdu; they both visited Lon-don to discuss with Liberal politicians what could be done about independence for Egypt. Mohammed Abdu was then bitter against the British. 'Do not attempt to do us any more good,' he said in a newspaper interview, 'your good has done us too much harm already.'[75] But later he decided that it was useless to try to get rid of the British, and that it was better to make use of them. He returned to Egypt to try to educate public opinion, reinterpret the Koran, improve education, and reform al-Azhar University. From his experience of the Arabi movement he did not believe that political revolution could be effective at that stage; first it was necessary to transform the attitude of mind of Egyptians, which he set out to do with untiring zeal. In 1899 he became Grand Mufti and was able to effect a great deal. He argued that the only way to reform was to tackle Egypt's failings through the people's religious sentiment. 'They have so long been motivated by religious factors', he wrote, 'that it has now become something like second nature to them'; the 'so-called literary education' introduced by Mohammed Ali had not moved them because it was divorced from religion.[76] Later Egyptian reformers tended to forget the importance of religion among the masses in Egypt. Abdu wanted use to be made of the knowledge of Europe and he himself read widely English and French works on ethics, history, sociology, education, and philosophy, but he saw clearly the danger that society might become divided. On the one hand were those who followed Europe and forgot Islam, because they considered that it was out of date; on the other were those who governed their life according to the laws and moral principles of Islam and ignored, indeed refused to have any contact with, the learning from the West. He attacked the methods of the Koranic schools which taught children to learn the Koran by heart without encouraging them to use their intelligence; Mohammed Abdu had run away from the religious school in Tanta where he had spent a year and a half 'without understanding anything at all because the teaching methods were so bad'.

Shaikh Abdu questioned the Muslim authorities (*Taklid*) on the interpretation of the Koran and of the Sayings or Traditions (*Hadith*) of the Prophet Mohammed, which had been accepted unchanged for centuries. 'I raised my voice', he wrote, 'to free the mind from the chains of belief on authority [*Taklid*]. . . . Islam declared openly that man was not created to be led by a halter, but that it is his nature to be guided by science and by signs of the universe and the indication of events.' He considered that it was the interpretation which had vitiated religion 'and if we continue to follow this method of blind acceptance, no one will be left who holds this religion'; but Islam could be made into 'the religion of reason, to which all the nations shall have recourse'. It was only because Shaikh Mohammed Abdu was held in such respect that he was able to argue effectively that the Koran and the Traditions should be reinterpreted for each genera-tion and to carry out his own reinterpretations against the criticism which came from the Muslim pundits of al-Azhar. 'His greatness of character impressed all who knew him. Because of his native dignity of bearing and his refusal to flatter or cajole anyone, even the great and influential, he was sometimes accused of pride. But in reality he was humble . . . and forgiving towards those who opposed him and thought to injure him. . . . Devotion to Islam was the controlling motive of his life.'[77]

Lord Cromer liked Mohammed Abdu and may well have been influenced by his arguments about the need for education; towards the end of his rule, belatedly, he began to pay attention to this important subject and appointed one of Mohammed Abdu's disciples, Saad Zaghlul (1860–1927), as Minister of Education. But on the question of Islam, Cromer reflected the views of most Westerners; he considered that the religion was 'politically and socially moribund; . . . its gradual decay cannot be arrested by any modern palliatives however skilfully they may be applied'.[78] He and others who have argued that Islam was a petrified religion had no understanding of it.

It is not Islam that is petrified, but its orthodox formulations, its systematic theology, its social apologetic. It is here that the dislocation lies, that the dissatisfaction is felt among a large proportion of its most educated and intelligent adherents and that the danger for its future is most evident. . . . That for the vast majority of Muslims the problem of dislocation has not yet arisen justifies the Ulama in refusing to be rushed into the hasty measures which the modernists prescribe; but the spread of modernism is a warning that re-formulation cannot be indefinitely shelved.[79]

Mohammed Abdu died in 1905 at the age of fifty-six, his commentary on the Koran left incomplete, but he had helped to start a revolution in thought and his creative ideas fell on fertile soil. 'No great work was completed in Egypt that his hand was not in it before any other hand', wrote Mohammed Rashid Rida who was to carry on his work, emphasizing the Islamic side of his doctrine.

There were, indeed, two sides to Shaikh Mohammed Abdu's teaching. He had argued that if there were a contradiction in the Koran or in the Traditions, 'reason must believe that the apparent sense was not intended'. Such arguments were taken up by those disciples who wished to accept the logic of Western reasoning. But Mohammed Abdu had been careful to try to define what could be questioned and what could not. He may not have realized fully the difficulties caused by introducing reason, for he believed that there could not, in fact, be a contradiction between reason and divine revelation. He pointed the way to resolving the problem, but it lay open to his many disciples to develop either of the two aspects of his teaching – the importance of reason or the importance of revelation in the Koran and in the Traditions.

POLITICAL REFORMERS

Among those who developed what might be called the educational side of Mohammed Abdu's teaching was Ahmad Lufti al-Sayyed (1872–1946), who had met al-Afghani in Constantinople and had been a disciple of Mohammed Abdu. His main concern was to protect the freedom of the individual, so that he or she could develop an independence of spirit and help create a true civilization; he agreed with Mohammed Abdu that one of the first reforms must be of the national character, but he thought that this could be done best by general education rather than through religion. It was necessary, he wrote, to be liberated 'from the curse of worshipping uncritically thoughts and ideas on authority', and to shatter 'the chains which have held our mind in bondage and the fantasies which have prevented us from benefiting from the new ideals'.

Lufti al-Sayyed was not surprised that villagers in Egypt hid criminals from the police and avoided helping the government; governments had been despotic and their agents had not worked for the welfare of the nation, 'so the people tacitly obstruct its decrees, even when it is clear that they are just'. Saad Zaghlul had said 'the people have looked at the government as a bird at the hunter, not as an army at its leader'. His brother, Ahmad Fathi Zaghlul, who translated a number of English and French books into Arabic, had written 'religious solidarity has gone and so have racial bonds. . . . We are so weak we do nothing for ourselves; we ask the govern-ment instead.' Lufti al-Sayyed considered that Cromer did much for

Egypt by improving the finances and the economic conditions, but that he had not tried to create any moral relationship between ruler and ruled. Cromer apparently did not believe that it was possible to do so: 'The difference between Eastern and Western habits of thought constitute a barrier interposed between the Egyptian and the Englishman almost as great as that resulting from differences of religion, ideas of government, and social customs.'[80]

It was written perhaps in the bitterness of his last years. Cromer had been on good terms with many Egyptians, including Mohammed Abdu and Saad Zaghlul, who kept a photograph of Cromer in his room alongside one of Abdu, of al-Afghani, and of Bismarck; indeed there was a time when Zaghlul thought it might be possible to combine British and Egyptian reformers to curb the power of the Khedive. The British had at one period been quite popular; indeed Saad Zaghlul's brother, Ahmad Fathi, translated a French book into Arabic called *A quoi tient la supériorité des Anglo-Saxons* by E.-R. Demolins, which had a vogue in Egypt.

LUFTI AL-SAYYED AND MUSTAPHA KAMIL

In his campaign for Egyptian independence Lufti al-Sayyed had begun by working with Mustapha Kamil (1874–1908), who is often described as the founder of modern Egyptian nationalism but there have been others, and it was Lufti al-Sayyed who worked out a comprehensive national ideology. He had been asked by Mustapha Kamil to edit the National Party newspaper *al-Liwa* ('The Standard'), but Lufti al-Sayyed broke with the National Party largely because of the Pan-Islam sentiments of Mustapha Kamil; he did not like such movements and considered that nationality should be territorial; Egyptians should take pride in their own history starting with the Pharaohs. That had produced an Egyptian personality which would not be overwhelmed by importations of ideas and institutions from the West.

An interesting example of this division among the politicians and the people was given in June 1906, over the Aqaba incident. It was to Egypt's interest to retain Aqaba, which was demanded by Turkey. The British authorities opposed the Turks with the approval of Egyptians such as Lufti al-Sayyed and Saad Zaghlul; but the Turkish claim was supported by Mustapha Kamil, and the country-people of Egypt. This divided loyalty was repeated during the First World War when Turkey threatened the Suez Canal. The case for the general view of the masses is admirably put in a letter, received by Lord Cromer during the Aqaba incident. It pointed out how Egyptians had every reason to hate the Turk but concluded: 'Though the Caliph was helpless as Bayazid, cruel as Murad or mad as Ibrahim, he is the shadow of God, and every Muslim must leap up at his call as the willing servant of his master, though the wolf may devour his child while he does his father's work.'[81]

Lufti al-Sayyed considered that such ideas were more damaging to the growth of Egyptian nationhood than the British occupation. To counter the Pan-Turk and Pan-Islam preachings of Mustapha Kamil, the disciples of Mohammed Abdu founded in 1907 the People's Party, known also as the Umma Party. Lufti al-Sayyed became its Secretary and Chief Editor of the Party newspaper, *al-Jarida*, through which he exercised great influence and earned the title of 'Teacher of the Generation'. In the same year the National Party was given a proper organization, and another political party was founded, controlled by the Khedive, and called the Party of Constitutional Reform.

Mustapha Kamil was a great orator and a national idol and, like Lufti al-Sayyed, he believed in the Nation-State, but his ideas were confused and he understood very little about traditional Muslim beliefs and education. He seemed to think that Islam was like Christianity and only concerned with faith and morals so that he was able to make such statements as: 'I believe that religion and nationalism are inseparable twins'; or again, 'he whose heart is possessed by religion would love his fatherland and sacrifice his goods and life for it'; but it was not clear which fatherland he meant. Mustapha Kamil preached, too, the brotherhood between Muslims and Copts and did much to help bring them together.

The demand for independence was gradually being organized and made popular by Mustapha Kamil's great oratorical powers. He regarded the British as the enemies of the Egyptians and he would not grant that Cromer had carried out useful reforms; without the British 'all reforms would have been carried out, and even better carried out'. In fact Cromer, although he did not believe in independence for Egyptians, helped the movement forward by allowing freedom of discussion in the Press. The Egyptian newspapers, of which there were many, were free, lively, and critical of the government, more so than they are today in Egypt. Mustapha Kamil himself owed Cromer his freedom to speak and write and also to the support of the Khedive Abbas Hilmi who had succeeded Tawfik.

Mustapha Kamil had relied on the help of the French who were bitter against the British, but he was disappointed when in 1898 Kitchener stopped their advance into the Sudan at Fashoda. He was also disappointed when the two countries established their *entente cordiale* in 1904. After that it was clear that Egyptians would have to win independence for themselves. There was one event which encouraged Mustapha Kamil and that was the victory of an Eastern nation, the Japanese, against the Russians in 1905, and he wrote a book about Japan called *The Rising Sun*. The point was noted, too, that it was a country with a democratic Constitution, which had defeated the Russian autocratic government; it was argued that this was yet another reason why Egypt should have a proper Constitution and Parliament. Kamil, in spite of his Pan-Islamic sentiments, had an intense feeling of patriotism for Egypt, 'the world's paradise', and in his speeches he tried to instil this patriotism in others. To him Egypt meant the Nile Valley and included the Sudan. After attending the opening of the Aswan Dam in 1902 he wrote: 'if in the future the English should construct reservoirs in the Sudan, Egypt would be at their mercy and would run the greatest dangers'. This fear remained in the minds of Egyptians. He believed that Britain would only abandon Egypt if sufficient pressure was exerted, and he tried to work up national feeling by his speeches and by organizing students' strikes which were to become a feature of Egyptian life during periods of tension. When he died in 1908 he was mourned throughout Egypt; Cromer had left the year before and was unmourned.

Lord Cromer did much to help Egypt's finances, irrigation, and general economic development. There has been discussion as to whether this could not have been achieved without the bombard/ ment of Alexandria and the killing of Egyptians in battle.

Thus, at the end of Cromerism, the capital value of the debt was much the same as at the beginning. What Cromerism can claim is that it saved Egypt from bankruptcy and from the consequent increase of foreign control, and gave it time to become so economic/ ally convalescent that it could bear the burden of the debt with/ out breaking the back of the Fellah.[82]

Egyptian nationalists complained that Cromer did not encourage education, nor delegate power to Egyptians, nor introduce political institutions. He did, however, allow Egyptians great freedom of expression and British administrators established high standards. 'The suppression of the [Arabi] revolt and establishment of British control', wrote Professor Gibb, 'while outwardly a political set/ back, in reality caused the Westernizing movement to broaden out and to flow into deeper channels. Cairo became the centre where all the active forces in the Muslim world met.'[83]

Cromer had never sympathized with the nationalists, but he had thought that at least the Fellaheen would understand what he had done – the great benefits he had given them by supplying water through the big irrigation projects. In the year before he left, however, there was a village tragedy which destroyed the former goodwill.

THE PIGEONS OF DENSHAWY VILLAGE

In June 1906, the Fellaheen of the village of Denshawy objected to British officers shooting their pigeons and this led to the death of a British officer and a villager. The special tribunal which tried the Fellaheen condemned four out of the fifty/two villagers to be executed and others to be beaten or sentenced to long terms of imprisonment with hard labour. Cromer was on leave and could not be contacted; he supported the decision afterwards, though he had serious misgivings as to the effect on public opinion. Few seemed to understand that the pigeons were kept by the villagers for ferti/ lizing the land with their guano; their dove/cots are to be seen still in the villages today. As early as the 1860s Lady Duff Gordon wrote from Luxor in protest against the English travellers who thought they had the right to shoot the pigeons which belonged to the villagers; one was shot by a visitor as it sat on her balcony. The author of 'Hints on Shooting' in *Murray's Hand-book on Egypt* (1880 edition) stated that the foreign gentleman 'is accustomed to go where he likes in pursuit of game: ripe standing crops offer no obstacle to him'. After the disaster which had caused a storm in Egypt, England, and Europe, no more was said in a 1907 guide-book than, 'sports-men should be careful about shooting pigeons in the near neighbour-hood of a village, as they are often alleged to be domestic ones'.[84]

It was this ignorance and lack of sensitivity – it could be called arrogance – with regard to the rights and feelings of the people that aroused their hostility. For instance, there had long been the double standards of the foreign speculators – one for Europeans and a lower one for Egyptians.

> In the many-sided impact of imperialism, it is the injury to self-respect that hurts most. It is the resentment aroused by spiritual humiliation that gives rise to an irrational response to rational exploitation. The apparently unreasonable, and certainly un-profitable, resistance of many of the world's underdeveloped countries today to Western business enterprise makes sense only in this context.[85]

Cromer himself had become very autocratic in his latter years in Cairo. One of his British colleagues wrote:

> *The virtues of patience are known,*
> *But I think, when put to the touch,*
> *The people of Egypt will own, with a groan,*
> *There's an evil in Baring too much.*

When in 1911 he published his *Modern Egypt* it aroused great dis-tress and hostility, not only for his unfavourable comments on Islam but also for his views that Egyptians would never be able to rule themselves; 'the ideal of the Muslim patriot is, in my opinion, incapable of realization'. He wanted Muslim or Christian, Euro-peans, Asiatics, and Africans 'to be fused into one self-governing body with an international Legislative Council', in which the European communities would have a strong position. It was an extraordinary idea; but he could look back at history and argue that for nearly twenty-five centuries – from the Persian Conquest of 525 BC until his day – the country had not been ruled by Egyptians, except for a short period known as the Restoration, the rulers had been Persians, Greeks, Turks, Kurds, Mameluke Circassians, and Ottoman Turks. But that is not how the nationalists looked at the question.

Cromer's successor, Sir Eldon Gorst, returned to the unpopular policy of encouraging the Khedive; Kitchener took over with a more liberal policy in 1913 and introduced a Legislative Assembly; but the outbreak of the First World War meant further control and more troops to occupy the country. The day after the outbreak of war in Europe, on 5 August 1914, the Egyptian Prime Minister signed a decree empowering the British to exercise the rights of war throughout Egypt. With the entry of Turkey into the war, martial law was declared and preparation made to defend the Suez Canal. There had been a proclamation that Egyptians would not be called on for defence but very soon they were ordered to guard the Suez Canal against their fellow-Muslims the Turks whom many pre-ferred to the British. In December, the British government declared a Protectorate over Egypt. The nationalists hated the war and hoped that Britain would lose it, otherwise there seemed no hope for in-dependence. The peasants suffered by having their animals and their crops taken; the army paid good prices but the money often did not reach them owing to middlemen; most-hated imposition of all, they were drafted into labour battalions (supposed to be volun-tary) for service in France and elsewhere. In 1917 came the Balfour Declaration – a unilateral decision that the Jews could establish a National Home in Palestine, a territory that belonged to the Arabs who were not consulted. The next year saw the important statement made by the President of the United States, Mr Woodrow Wilson, on self-determination, included in his fourteen points for a post-war settlement; that raised the hopes of Egyptian nationalists. But in November 1918, Saad Zaghlul and other leading Egyptians were at first refused permission to go to the Peace Conference in Paris to plead the cause of Egyptian independence; the British government had many problems to deal with and thought that Egypt could wait. It did not see why there should be any cause for complaint for, it was argued, Egypt had been saved by the British Army from invasion by the Turks from the east and by the Senussi from the west; Egypt had also accumulated a balance of over one hundred and fifty million pounds in five years of war. To the Egyptians it was galling to see representatives of Syria, Arabia, and of Cyprus being allowed to send representatives to the Peace Conference without question, and to see Syria granted what amounted to independence in November 1918. In Egypt the British Army continued to maintain martial law; they had to deal with the withdrawal of thousands of troops stretching from Cairo into Asia Minor and supplies from Egypt continued to be needed.

They were logical arguments from the British point of view but Egyptians had their own logic; they were not prepared to be patient. Saad Zaghlul and his Wafd Party had a widespread organization throughout the country and refused the British military order to stop propaganda against Britain. In March 1919, Saad Zaghlul and others were arrested and sent to Malta. But Zaghlul in exile was an even more powerful factor than he had been while in Egypt and revolution suddenly broke out throughout the country; railways in some areas were torn up, stations burnt, British troops murdered on trains, and European civilians killed.

The British were surprised and impressed by the rebellion, but the government continued to believe that Egypt wanted its help and protection; it clung to the Protectorate formula and to martial law. Zaghlul, now an angry and bitter man, was allowed to return. There was more rioting and more deaths, and Saad Zaghlul, Mustapha Nahas, and other Wafd leaders were exiled to the Seychelles.

Sir Edmund Allenby (later Lord Allenby), the High Commissioner, realized a new deal was needed and forced the hand of the British government to make their Declaration of 28 February 1922. This terminated the Protectorate and recognized Egypt 'as an independent sovereign State', but there were four important reserved points which remained the responsibility of Britain: security of communications of the British Empire, defence, protection of foreign investments and of minorities, and the Sudan. It was qualified independence; the British Army remained with its headquarters in the Citadel dominating Cairo and with troops on the Suez Canal. There was more trouble and more British soldiers were killed.

On 19 April 1923 a Constitution was published; Sultan Ahmed Fuad became King. A Senate and a Chamber of Deputies were established; martial law was ended at last, and Saad Zaghlul with the other Wafdist leaders returned from exile. Zaghlul won an over-whelming majority at the elections and became Prime Minister in January 1924. His intransigence and arrogance aroused great hostility among many political opponents; on his departure for London to negotiate with Mr Ramsay Macdonald, the Prime Minister, Zaghlul was nearly assassinated at the station by a young effendi. In London he failed to obtain full independence; in Egypt murder and outrages continued against British civil servants and the army, and against Egyptian ministers and officials. In the Sudan, Egyptian officers had planned a rising and there was serious trouble; in Cairo on 19 November 1924, Sir Lee Stack, Governor-General of the Sudan and Sirdar of the Egyptian Army, was murdered. Allenby struck back by ordering the withdrawal of Egyptian troops from the Sudan, thus modifying the terms of the Condominium, and imposing a fine of half a million pounds. It was also decided that the Sudan should be granted the right to use more Nile water; many in Britain considered that this was not suitable to include in an ultimatum.

Subsequent years witnessed a battle between the Wafd and their opponents, backed by King Fuad, with the new High Commis-sioner, Lord Lloyd, trying to fill the role of a new Cromer. Saad Zaghlul died in 1927 and Mustapha Nahas Pasha became leader of the Wafd; under the threat of an expansionist Fascist Italy in Libya and in Ethiopia, the Wafd signed a treaty with Britain in 1936.

6 Reason versus revelation

BOTH THE NATIONAL and the People's Party were supported throughout the country much more widely than the Arabi-Afghani movement had been. Their secular Western ideas appealed to a new middle class of journalists and lawyers, Government officials and students, who understood the appeal of nationalism and independence.

The masses in the country districts did not understand that appeal, but they had good negative reasons for giving their support because of their sufferings during the First World War.

The 1919 Revolution had been so sudden and so violent that even the Egyptian nationalists were puzzled; as already stated, Tawfik al-Hakim was later to try to explain the phenomenon by a reference back to Pharaonic times. The Liberal Nationalists of the 1920s explained the revolt by the convenient argument that the masses had understood the message about nationalism and independence and had been moved to action. But these ideas were still entirely alien to them. The revolt was anti-foreign and religious, as it had been against Bonaparte's French troops in Cairo, prompted by the emotions of the *jihad*, or holy war, against the foreign infidel who dared to occupy a land of the Believers. That might seem an over-statement to those who have experienced only the friendliness of Egyptians to foreigners in times of tranquillity; but anyone who has seen rioting in the towns and the country-side knows how quickly violence can develop when emotions have been roused.

Very little attempt was made by political leaders to explain the new concepts. The Constitution of 1923, for instance, was a con-tract between King and people based on that of Belgium; it was foreign and non-Egyptian. While stating that Islam was the religion of the State a number of the articles were drawn from the civil code and were at variance with Islamic law and usage; to try to cover this, vague phrases were introduced, such as 'in conformity with the usages established in Egypt', or 'the laws of the Egyptian people'. This ambivalence throughout much of law-making was not always successful in calming the opposition of the orthodox; certain clauses intended to restrict polygamy, for instance, had to be omitted because of the outcry aroused; in 1943 and 1945 a draft law to impose limitations on the right to divorce had to be abandoned.

THE CALIPHATE

The Liberal Nationalists also tended to ignore Islamic political concepts, such as that of the Caliphate and of Pan-Islam. The reforms carried out by Mustapha Kemal Ataturk in Turkey, for instance, shocked not only the orthodox Muslims there but also in Egypt. In 1924 the Turkish National Assembly abolished the Caliphate altogether. Mustapha Kemal argued that it was not a spiritual office but a political one, and as there could no longer be a united Muslim State it ceased to have any meaning in the days of nationalism. There was an outcry among orthodox Muslims and two years later the Egyptian Ulama called a Congress to discuss the question, presided over by the Rector of al-Azhar University. It was concluded that the Caliphate had both temporal and spiritual powers and it was hoped that a Caliph could be elected at some future time.

A contrary view was given by a young liberal, Ali Abd al-Raziq, who published a book called *al-Islam* in 1925; he argued that there was no system of government which was specifically Islamic, and that Mohammed's role had been as a Prophet dealing with the spiritual side. He argued that the first Caliph, Abu Bakr, had set up an Arab State concerned with Arab interests, and the idea that the Caliph had spiritual leadership as well, had been encouraged by absolute rulers for their own purposes; Muslims were free to choose whatever form of government or political system suited them. The orthodox reaction to the book was strong; great trouble

127

was taken in refuting it and the Ulama of al-Azhar also forbade the author to hold any public religious office and he retired into private life. In refuting Abd al-Raziq's arguments Shaikh Mohammed Bakhit of al-Azhar wrote: 'The Islamic religion is based on the pursuit of domination and power and strength and might, and the refusal of any law which is contrary to its Sharia and its divine law, and the rejection of any authority the wielder of which is not charged with the execution of its edicts.'[86] The Shaikh considered that Abd al-Raziq and other liberal writers were trying to abolish the Sharia laws, which stood over and above the government, and were necessary in order to prevent oppression and anarchy; anarchy would be the result, he wrote, of using reason and self-interest to decide on forms of government.

DR TAHA HUSAYN

The strength of the orthodox leaders was shown again in 1926 when they defended themselves against the attacks of the most remarkable and the most widely known of Egyptian philosophers, writers, and educationists – Dr Taha Husayn. He also had been influenced by Mohammed Abdu, some of whose lectures he had attended at al-Azhar. In 1926 he published a book *On Pre-Islamic Poetry* which sounded innocuous, but in fact was a devastating attack on the methods in the past of interpreting the Koran and the Traditions, derived to a great extent from the meaning of the words of Pre-Islamic Arab poetry. He argued that the poetry should not be used for interpretation:

> Undoubtedly it was tailored and invented all of a piece so that the Ulama might prove by it what they had set out to prove. . . . I want to introduce in literature that philosophical method for investigating the truth of things, which Descartes formulated at the beginning of the modern era. . . . We must not heed the question of what might contradict that nationality or that religion; we must be bound by nothing except the methods of true scientific investigation.

Taha Husayn argued that the Koranic stories about Abraham and Ishmael had been made up; there was also 'another sort of invented

128

poetry which has been attributed not to human Arabs, but to pre-Islamic Arab *jinns*', and he went on to ridicule the whole conception of *jinns*. He was more direct in his attacks than Mohammed Abdu, who had done his utmost to avoid shocking the orthodox; Mohammed Abdu, for instance, did not condemn outright the idea of *jinns*, but put forward the ingenious theory that microbes, which had been discovered under the microscope and could be good or bad, might be a species of *jinns*. That was acceptable to many of the orthodox who argued that the Koran contained all knowledge, including that of the sciences.

Taha Husayn was born in 1889 in Upper Egypt and had become totally blind at the age of three, but after studying at the local school he went at the age of thirteen to al-Azhar where he stayed for ten years being fortunate enough to have a good teacher. Lufti al-Sayyed who had been appointed Rector of Cairo University, had encouraged him to learn Greek and Latin; Taha Husayn also attended lectures at the Sorbonne in Paris and at the Collège de France, in history, philosophy, psychology, and sociology. He became Professor of Classical Literature, at the Cairo University, translating into Arabic, Aristotle, classic plays of Sophocles and other works; he was then transferred to the Faculty of Arabic Letters. He wrote two weekly essays in *al-Jarida* and various didactic novels, so that by the time he published *On Pre-Islamic Poetry* at the age of thirty-nine he was widely known, not only in Egypt but also abroad.

The uproar over his book became a *cause célèbre* and there was a heated debate in Parliament which nearly led to the fall of the Government. The Opposition accused Taha Husayn of undermining the faith of Islam and argued that, as the Egyptian University was paid by the State, he should be dismissed and the book suppressed. The book was withdrawn and Dr Taha Husayn resigned from the University but the authorities stood by him and refused to accept the resignation. Rashid Rida considered that Taha Husayn had 'established his apostasy from Islam'; the Rector of al-Azhar and others brought legal action against Taha Husayn. He was tried on the charge of undermining the State religion, but the Court dismissed the case after a careful review of the charges. Certain of the offending passages were removed and the book was published again in 1927 and called *On Pre-Islamic Literature*. But in 1931 when Ismail Sidky, the Prime Minister, wished to get rid of Dr Taha Husayn for political reasons, the case was reopened and he was dismissed from the University; Lufti el-Sayyed, who was still Rector, resigned in protest.

Dr Taha Husayn argued in his writings that Egypt was a Mediterranean country. Islam had assimilated Greek and Persian civilizations and she could do the same with the European; the only reason for the differences today was that Europe's renaissance had been in the fifteenth century and Egypt's in the nineteenth. Neither Dr Taha Husayn nor Lufti al-Sayyed were apprehensive that Egyptian or Arab civilization would be overwhelmed by the West. For Lufti al-Sayyed there was the Egyptian personality or 'Pharaonic core', and also the vigorous and rich Arabic language; 'To my mind', he wrote, 'the preservation of the language and the enthusiasm for serving it by reinvigorating its life through new styles and idioms are proof that a nation has personality and self-respect.'

Egyptian writing, however, was still concerned with the philosophic question of Egypt's identity, the position of Islam in a secular State, or the political question of getting rid of the British; very little attention was paid to the important problem of economics and how to run a newly independent country. For, qualified as was her independence, Egypt had gained the right to manage her own internal affairs; there was a King, a Constitution, and a Parliament. Further political advance was made with the signing of the Anglo-Egyptian Treaty of 1936 and in 1937 Egypt became a member of the League of Nations. In the same year the Montreux Convention ended some of the anomalies of the Capitulations, though it was several more years before they were finally abolished.

LIBERALS ENCOURAGED

The Egyptian liberals considered that progress was being made. There was a theory of government and of social behaviour, and a consistent way of life seemed to be emerging. 'I felt, as other Egyptians did', wrote Dr Taha Husayn, '. . . that Egypt was beginning a new period of her life: she had obtained some of her rights, and must now set herself to important duties and heavy responsibilities.'[87]

Yet even the liberal leaders did not readily understand the purpose of the Constitution or realize that it was a framework to which improvements could be made; they ignored 'the mechanics of democracy'.

> The legalistic approach became an attitude towards the Constitution, not unlike that of the Ulama to the Sharia, whereby the Constitution was viewed as a doctrine or a set of rules, extrinsic to and above society . . . rather than as a combination of 'political engineering' derived by mankind from experience. . . . Political principles appeared to them as self-evident ethical imperatives, and political behaviour as simply bad or good moral conduct.[88]

The weight of past methods of Islamic teaching still weighed on them – even on the intellectuals. While they were trying to make these new ideas and institutions a part of Egyptian life, there came a serious set-back.

CONFUSION IN POLITICS AND PHILOSOPHY

At the time that Egypt was trying to pursue democratic ideas borrowed from Europe, many Europeans themselves became uncertain as to whether democracy was the right goal; the Fascists, Nazis, and Communists were all contemptuous of parliamentary government and even in France and Britain voices were raised against the system. Saad Zaghlul, although he had shown himself intransigent and dictatorial in his relations with other politicians, was a great leader and his death in 1927 was a severe loss to Egypt. The government was disrupted by a series of unhappy conflicts between the King and the Wafd, while the British threw in their weight first on one side and then on the other. There was not only confusion in politics but also in the theories of the Egyptian philosophers and writers.

In spite of the continued opposition of the orthodox Ulama, the Egyptian liberal intellectuals had moved away from the idea of divine sanction in ethics and relied on conscience and responsibility to society. Ahmad Amin's *Book of Ethics* was published in 1929 and became a textbook for secondary schools and the teachers' college; he based his arguments on the theory of Kant's intuition – that there was an inner force which revealed what deeds were good or evil in themselves. It was not an easy concept for anyone to follow and especially difficult for those who had been brought up on ethical rules laid down by religious authorities. It meant a complete division in the system of education; some were given religious teaching and others secular.

This was the division that Shaikh Mohammed Abdu had considered it was essential to avoid, and it would seem that Dr Taha Husayn realized the danger of pursuing reason to the exclusion of everything else and therefore changed his attitude, though some have suggested that it was the violent attacks of the orthodox which made him modify his views. During the climax of the ferment caused by the publication in 1926 of his book *On Pre-Islamic Poetry*, Dr Taha Husayn had written a letter to the Director of the Egyptian University asserting that he was a true Muslim and believed in Allah, the Koran, the Angels, and the Day of Judgment. During his trial in the Court he had been asked to explain the contradiction between the letter, which had been made public, and the view expressed in his book. He had replied:

> Every one of us can discover within himself two distinct personalities, one a rational personality and the other a sentient personality. . . . What is there, then, to prevent the first from being scholarly, inquisitive and critical, and the other from being a believing, assured personality, aspiring towards the highest ideals.

He elaborated this dual approach in a three-volume work on Mohammed, *In the Margin of the Prophet's Tradition*, the first volume of which appeared in 1934. The modernists, he now argued, should not trust only in reason, nor should they try to destroy the legends and myths of the people, on the argument that they corrupted the mind. This was, of course, what he had himself been doing before. 'These legends and tales', now wrote Dr Taha Husayn, 'do not satisfy reason and are not acceptable to logic . . . but the sensibilities, emotions and imagination of the people and their *naïveté* . . . make them like and desire these legends and seek in them relief from the burdens of life.' This was true, and it was certainly time that the intellectuals began to consider what happened to the minds and emotions of a highly religious people if you stripped Islam of the human stories some of which were sacred, because they were re-garded as part of what God had revealed through the Prophet Mohammed. But in extending his sympathy to the people in this way, Taha Husayn was destroying the basis of his argument as a philosopher. There were the truths approved by science and reason on the one hand, and on the other were legends presented 'to the heart' which stimulated 'good intentions', and they were both now stated to be valid. 'What grounds did Taha have to defend his own legends or to criticize those of anyone else, once he had exempted them from the rational principle of validation ?'[89] Dr Taha Husayn had returned to the problem which had faced Shaikh Mohammed Abdu, who had tried to resolve the dichotomy by making a detailed examination of the Koran and the Traditions through reason, but still leaving much to revelation. But it was not really resolved for there remained a division between those who worked on the basis of logic and reason and those whose hearts and emotions were stirred by belief.

REINTERPRETING HISTORY

Another attempt to deal with this problem was made by Dr Mohammed Husayn Haykal (1889–1956), who was President of the Senate, Leader of the Liberal Constitutionalist Party, and Editor of its newspaper (*al-Siyasah*). He went back to Mohammed Abdu's thesis of separating what was based on revelation and what was based on reason, but was not very successful. In his *Life of Mohammed* published in 1935, Haykal argued that man needed religion to establish his relationship with the universe; then he set out to try to prove that such things as Angels and Mohammed's visit to Heaven from Jerusalem could be explained scientifically. He went on to glorify Islam and praise the Prophet Mohammed with arguments which did not stand up to the standards demanded, for example, by Dr Taha Husayn, who had outlined the methods of true scientific investigation which might lead to changing history, 'or what had hitherto been regarded as history'. But Haykal's historical method in his *Life of Mohammed* was not scientific; by changing his ground he set out to justify various actions which were not in fact justifiable on the arguments he put forward. 'Each issue was considered in isolation and the same principles and facts were interpreted differently on different occasions to suit the purpose immediately at hand.'[90] Haykal, who had been one of the reformers, was accused of having become a reactionary. His book was extremely popular because many of his readers were gratified and relieved to find that orthodox doctrine could be shown to be true; they did not notice, or want to notice, the sophistry involved.

THE ROMANTIC INFLUENCE

It was the rewriting of history by such authors that prompted Professor Gibb to state that they were doing 'a profound disservice to Islam. . . . They have fastened on it still more firmly the shackles of the romantic imagination and encouraged it to interpret history in terms of the capricious impulses of the moment.'[91] He argued that the nineteenth-century Muslim reformers had studied Europe at a time when the Romantic movement was at its height; they had taken back with them, 'the imaginative legacy of romanticism, which had indeed been stimulated in Europe by the influence of Arabic literature in the Middle Ages and again by the popularity of *The Arabian Nights* in the eighteenth century'. This meant that reason had tended to be subordinated to imagination and subjective standards put in the place of objective ones; 'in conjunction with the belief in evolution it led to a rejection of all ultimates'. In Europe this tendency had been countered by 'scientific determinism and the growth of the historical method. . . . The immense revolution in historical thought in the West in the nineteenth century has not penetrated into the Muslim world.' It was disconcerting to find, for instance, that modernists in Egypt seized on 'any pronouncements by Western writers, no matter how ill-founded, uncritical or partisan, which chime in with their own sentiments or flatter their pride'. At the same time Professor Gibb pointed out that in the West people forgot too easily 'how recent and how limited is the spread of the dispassionate examination of facts'. He also considered that there did exist in Egypt true followers of Mohammed Abdu and that 'the evolutionary concept of historical development is slowly broadening out and overleaping the limitations set upon it by the traditional orthodox doctrine. But this is only a first step and the struggle against fundamentalism has still to be fought.'

ATTACK ON THE WEST

Mohammed Husayn Haykal took up the charge that he had be come a reactionary in another book called *In the Birthplace of Revelation*. Here he made a distinction between the 'rational life' of the West, which he accepted, and the spiritual life, which he rejected, as well as such things as nationalism; 'the glitter of Western civilization has caused us to forget the deadly germs that this nationalist idea carries for any civilization that rests on it exclusively . . . a nation whose present is not connected with its past is bound to lose its way. . . . Hence the chasm which had kept widening between the masses of the peoples of the East and those who argued that we should ignore our past and turn with all our might in the Western direction.' His influence on other writers and on the younger generation of students was considerable and by attacking the philo sophy and principles of the West he was taking away the only principles on which Egyptians could base their progress towards a modern State, principles in which he formerly believed. He seems to have been persuaded into this new line of argument by his desire to defend Islam, which he considered was still under attack from the West: 'Even though the Crusades have ended . . . the fanaticism of the Church against Mohammed has remained most powerful to the present day. . . . Many philosophers and writers in Europe and America, although unconnected with the Church, have also taken up on their own account the fanaticism against Mohammed.' He used the argument that Western culture had failed because mankind was not happy and therefore looked towards the East for spirituality.

The new trend initiated by Haykal added to the confusion and has been well described by Mr Safran: 'The attempt to reconcile reason and revelation ended up as an apology for Islam which not only damaged the integrity of reason, but also weakened the second guiding principle by its denigration of Western culture, and thus denied subsequent intellectual activity any common centre of gravity.' Dr Taha Husayn was disturbed to find that Haykal's writings exercised great influence, and that in defending the need to follow the West, Taha Husayn was now in a minority, whereas before he had been in the vanguard of an important movement. 'This talk of a spiritual East is sheer nonsense', he wrote. 'Egyptians who deride European culture and praise the spirituality of the East are joking, and they know it. . . . Nevertheless, their arguments are dangerous and demoralizing, particularly to the youth.' It was true, he wrote, that the Near East had been the cradle of religions and the Europeans had taken from these religions as had the people of the Near East, 'can these religions be spirit in the East and matter in the West ? . . . Let us admit the truth and banish hypocrisy; only by eagerly welcoming the modern civilization can we have true peace of mind and a wholesome attitude to the realities of life. . . . The world has struggled for hundreds of years to attain the present stage of progress; it is within our power to reach it within a short time. Woe to us if we do not seize the opportunity.'[92]

35 Mohammed Ali (1769–1848) was ruler of Egypt in the early nineteenth century. A lithograph by David Roberts of Mohammed Ali with English naval officers.

36 (*left below*) Lady Lucie Duff Gordon, the nineteenth-century writer, lived in Egypt for seven years. A lithograph by Barnett Freedman.

37 The Khedive Ismail who ruled Egypt from 1863–70 was severely criticized in many of Lady Duff Gordon's shrewd and observant letters. A contemporary engraving.

38 (*above*) One of the first Egyptian nationalists who led a revolt against the Khedive Tawfik was Ahmed Arabi (1839–1914). The British finally defeated him at the Battle of Tell el-Kebir in 1882. A contemporary engraving.

39 (*right*) Ahmed Arabi receiving his despatches. From a contemporary engraving.

40 (*right above*) Jamal al-Din al-Afghani (1839–97) was a revolutionary reformer of Islam who attained much influence throughout Egypt and the Muslim world.

41 (*right below*) Shaikh Mohammed Abdu (1849–1905) was a prominent nationalist and a reformer of the Islamic religion.

42 In 1869 the Suez Canal
was opened with a fantastic
and expensive festival in the
presence of the Empress
Eugénie. A contemporary engraving.

43 Lord Cromer (Evelyn
Baring) (1841–1917) was
British Consul-General and
virtual ruler of Egypt from
1883 to 1907.

44 Earl Kitchener of Khartum (1850–1916) who had long service with the army in Egypt became British Agent in 1914. As the two main outposts of the British Empire were India and Egypt this contemporary cartoon is entitled 'The Rival Enchantresses — Egypt and India'.

45 Lord Edmund Allenby (1861–1936) was British High Commissioner in Egypt from 1919 to 1925 and was responsible for the Declaration of Independence in 1922.

46 (*left above*) A Krupp field-gun manned by Egyptians defending the port of Alex-andria before the bombardment by the British in 1882. A contemporary engraving.

47 (*below*) Egyptian soldiers clearing the streets of Arab looters in Alexandria.

48 (*above*) The bombard‑
ment of Alexandria by the
British Navy in July 1882.

49 (*right*) After occupation
British marines arrested
Arabs in the streets of
Alexandria.

50 (*left above*) Saad Zaghlul (1860–1927), the Egyptian nationalist leader twice deported by the British, became the first Prime Minister of Egypt in 1924.

51 (*left below*) Lufti al-Sayyed (1872–1946) by his philosophy and teachings was one of the main progenitors of Egyptian independence.

52 Dr Taya Husayn (b. 1889) a colleague of Lufti al-Sayyed and much influenced by European ideas, has had a considerable influence on the religious and philosophical ideas in Egypt.

7 Nasser's Revolution

ONE OF THE EFFECTS of the Anglo-Egyptian Treaty of 1936 was that Britain paid more attention to the improvement of the Egyptian Army, and the Wafd Party, which wished to gain popularity, made recruitment to the Military Academy more democratic. Several young men who joined before the Second World War were to play principal roles in the Revolution of 1952 and Gamal Abdel Nasser was one of them.[93]

He was an Upper Egyptian, or Saidi; the grandson of a Fellah and the son of a post-office official who married the daughter of a Saidi. Gamal was born in 1918 and for eight years from the age of ten went to secondary schools in Helwan, Alexandria, and Cairo. Towards the end of his school career he became involved in politics; he read everything he could find of nineteenth-century Egyptian writers such as al-Afghani, Shaikh Mohammed Abdu, Mustapha Kamil, and Lufti al-Sayyed; he read Rousseau, Voltaire, Dickens, Hugo, and the lives of Julius Caesar, Alexander, Bonaparte, and of Gandhi. He considered joining the Wafd, or the Green Shirts modelled on the Italian Fascists, but neither satisfied him and the Communists held no attraction. 'Where is dignity?' he wrote to a friend in 1935. 'Where is nationalism? Where is what one can call the activity of youth? It has all disappeared and the nation lies asleep like the inhabitants of a cave. Who can wake them up, these miserable creatures who are not even aware of their own condition?'[94] Idealism had gone out of politics during the confused years between the two world wars. The Fellaheen were oppressed by the landowners, many of the Wafd Party politicians were corrupt, elections were rigged, and Parliament did very little effective business. The young King Faruk, who had succeeded his father in 1936, did not fulfil the promise expected; no guidance was given by King, politicians, or writers. Egyptian advance towards independence had been arrested and there was renewed frustration.

When Gamal Abdel Nasser joined the Military Academy in 1937 he found friends, some of Fellah origin, who were eager to try to achieve the renaissance of Egypt. Their main concern was to plan to get rid of the British, the landowners, and the Pashas. After graduating from the Military Academy Gamal Abdel Nasser was posted as a Second Lieutenant to Mankabad near Assiut where Anwar al-Sadat and Zakariya Muhieddin had also been posted. In 1939 he asked to be sent to the Sudan where he was joined by his friend Abdul Hakim Amer and was promoted Lieutenant. There were already the beginnings of a Revolutionary movement among the young officers of the army which centred round Gamal Abdel Nasser, because of his ability and calm personality. But while he was away in the Sudan the most active officer in Cairo seems to have been the energetic and impetuous Anwar al-Sadat.

REVOLUTIONARY SOCIETY FOUNDED

It is interesting that in Anwar al-Sadat's account of Gamal Abdel Nasser's background prominence is given to what Lufti al-Sayyed described as the Egyptian or Pharaonic core:

> Gamal's convictions were deep-rooted. He was a true son of the Said. He was passionately attached to the land of his origin, and his conversation was sown with proverbs and sayings from his native province. Said, the old Thebaid of the ancient Egyptians, is a beautiful and noble province. The great forces of nature hold sway there – the Nile and the earth which it waters. The men of Said are strong. It is a country of old legends and high deeds. It is a cradle of good workers, soldiers and stalwart men faithful to the ways of their ancestors. On a rocky eminence in the heart of this province, Mankabad perches like an eagle's nest in a narrow plain enclosed by granite hills.

It could be an account of the birthplace of Thutmosis III. There,

146

at the beginning of 1939, 'the officers of Mankabad founded a secret revolutionary society dedicated to the task of liberation'. Al-Sadat's account of Gamal Abdel Nasser is what might be expected: 'If we started a light-hearted conversation, it was invariably Gamal Abdel Nasser who interrupted to bring us back to graver topics. . . . His message to us was this: "We must fight imperialism, monarchy and feudalism, because we are opposed to injustice, oppression and slavery."'[95]

CONTACTS WITH ITALIANS AND GERMANS

When the Second World War broke out in 1939 the British Army once more controlled Egyptian affairs, but there was a great deal of intrigue with Italian and German agents; the young Egyptian nationalists called it 'patriotism' while the British military called it 'treason'. King Faruk had links with the Italians and the Young Officers, such as Anwar al-Sadat, had contacts with the Germans; 'We made contact with the German headquarters in Libya and we acted in complete harmony with them', wrote Anwar al-Sadat in *Revolt on the Nile*. 'For the intervention of Egypt could not take the form of an unsupported internal uprising. . . . But if a junction could be effected between Egyptian insurgents and Axis troops, our war would become an international affair.' He described the German attempt during the war to plan the escape from Egypt of General Aziz al-Masri, regarded as the spiritual father of the Young Officers' movement. A German plane landed in Egypt according to plan, but the General's car broke down on the way to the secret rendezvous. Al-Sadat also related the story of the two young German officers, sent as agents by Field-Marshal Rommel, who lived for some time on a house-boat in Cairo but had too many women visitors and were betrayed to the British. Such was the state of feeling in Egypt that it was not difficult for the Young Officers to infiltrate the army. 'Sections were formed in every branch of the Army', wrote al-Sadat. 'Each member had the right to recruit new members and was responsible for their conduct. Thus, each of us formed a new revolutionary cell around him. Soon there was a militant organization covering the entire country. Members used secret signs and passwords. . . . Gamal's wisdom preserved us from premature action and from many dangerous adventures.'

The British authorities knew of the unrest in the army, but they did not realize the extent of it. They also knew that the King was pro-Italian in sympathy. Sir Miles Lampson (Lord Killearn), the British Ambassador, made critical remarks which were passed to the Palace and the King retorted with references to the Ambassador's Italian wife, daughter of Dr Aldo Castellani; there was no love lost between them. When the Italians declared war in June 1940, the Ambassador insisted on the dismissal of the Prime Minister, Aly Maher Pasha, who was popular because he was pro-Axis.

The situation was critical for the British; Alexandria was bombed and the Italians had penetrated Egyptian territory as far as Tobruk. The hopes of the nationalist element in Egypt were raised when Rashid al-Gailani carried out a temporarily successful *coup d'état* in Iraq. It was essential to the British that the government in power should be friendly to the Allied cause. At the beginning of February 1942, Rommel's armoured divisions were advancing on Benghazi and there were student demonstrations in the streets calling on Rommel and shouting 'we are Rommel's soldiers'.[96] It was decided by the British that only the Wafd led by Mustapha Nahas would meet the requirements of controlling the King and the country, but the King was unwilling and the British Ambassador issued an ultimatum which was rejected.

ATTACK ON THE KING

The British Ambassador, with the General Officer Commanding British troops and an escort of armoured cars arrived at the Palace at nine p.m. on 4 February 1942, and forced their way to the King who gave in. This was regarded by nationalists as an insult to their King and to Egypt and caused high emotion. 'What is to be done', wrote Gamal Abdel Nasser to a friend the next day, 'now that the blow has been struck and we have taken it lying down.' General Mohammed Neguib, who was later to be called on to lead the Young Officers' revolt, was so shocked that he wanted to leave the army:

We seized power because we could no longer endure the humilia-
tions to which we, along with the rest of the Egyptian people,
were being subjected. For most of us the breaking-point was our
inexcusable defeat in Palestine, but for some of us it occurred
much earlier. My own breaking-point was reached in 1942, when
King Faruk surrendered to the then British Ambassador, Sir
Miles Lampson (now Lord Killearn), after his palace had been
surrounded with troops and tanks.[97]

The British government and Lord Killearn were criticized in
Britain, too, for this high-handed action; but from the British point
of view of helping to win the war, it was successful. The Wafd
won a big majority at the elections held in March and Mustapha
Nahas, the Prime Minister, kept Egypt on the side of the Allies for
the next two years, never weakening even when the Axis forces
under Rommel reached Alamein within about sixty miles of Alexandria. From the point of view of the Egyptian nationalists, such as
the Young Officers, it was remarkably short-sighted to think that
they would have been better off under a Nazi régime or that they
would have been likely to get rid of the Germans if they had won
the war. It was true, however, that the Wafd Party had lost its fire
and integrity and was controlled by wealthy landowners many of
whom were corrupt or indifferent.

While the British Ambassador was out of the country, the Wafd
was dismissed in October 1944, and Ahmed Maher Pasha became
Prime Minister, eager to carry out his wish to bring Egypt into the
war on the side of the Allies. Having announced this decision in
the Chamber of Deputies, the Prime Minister was on the way to
the Senate when he was assassinated, either by Ahmed Husayn's
extremist group, the *Misr-el-Fatat*, or, more probably, by a member
of the Muslim Brothers. He was succeeded by Mahmoud Fahmy
al-Nokrashi Pasha.

HASAN AL-BANNA

The Muslim Brothers ('Ikhwan al-Muslimun') had been started in
1928 by Hasan al-Banna, a young school-teacher in Ismailia. As a

schoolboy he had seen something of the 1919 Revolt and was shocked to see the difference between the way that the foreigner lived as compared to the Egyptian. He decided, therefore, that his mission was to liberate the Nile Valley and then other Arab countries from all foreigners. The movement acquired a tremendous following because he based it on the Koran; that was to be the Constitution, a way of life, and method of government. Egyptians were enthusiastic because at last they were presented with a programme which was part of their past and of their beliefs. This gave them pride and self-respect and for the Fellaheen the Koran was the only learning they had and the only solace in their misery. They abhorred the extrava-gant living of the foreigners and the 'shamelessness' of their women, contrary to the simple life set out in their holy book, which was to them a revelation from God through Mohammed his Prophet.

Hasan al-Banna shared their simple faith that the Koran ex-plained everything and believed that through it the country could win its own renaissance. As a boy he had been passionately religious and loved to organize societies; one of them was called 'The Society for the Prevention of Sin'; he would run to see that the *muezzin* had risen in time for the call to prayer and then knock on the neighbours' doors to make sure that they had heard it and were saying their prayers. He changed little as a young man when he founded his Society, for he sent letters to the King and rulers of Egypt and other Muslim countries, exhorting them to lead a pure life; congresses were held in Cairo and missions sent to other countries where branches were established. He was a fine orator and had a flair for organization. He had been a disciple of Rashid Rida, who had carried on the Islamic side of Shaikh Mohammed Abdu's teaching, so that the Muslim Brothers could to some extent be described as descendants, but their teaching was far less liberal than that of Shaikh Abdu, and he would certainly have disapproved of their political and terrorist activities.

By the time that the Second World War broke out the Muslim Brothers had become a powerful religio-political organization with arms hidden in different parts of the country and a well-trained terrorist wing. It could not be ignored by the Young Officers'

Revolutionary Committee; contact was made and a combined plan discussed, but Hasan al-Banna, 'The Supreme Guide' as he was called, wanted to keep arrangements in his own hands. The plan was put forward by the Revolutionary Committee through Anwar al-Sadat: a military *coup d'état* was to place Aly Maher again in power; the Egyptian Army would 'harry' the British forces and join up with the Axis troops 'and the fate of the British Empire would be sealed'.[98] There were periods when a chaotic situation in Cairo might have done great harm to the Allied cause, but if the *coup d'état* had been successful, the chance of full independence for Egypt would also have been sealed.

While some of the Young Officers were thinking on these un-realistic lines, many young Zionists had joined the British Army to learn the profession of fighting, not only because they regarded the Germans as their enemies, but also to train themselves for the battle for Palestine. Egyptian nationalists found it almost impossible to see beyond the problem of getting rid of the British; once they had done that they could move on to other things. The British government was not prepared to make any more concessions than those already made under the 1936 Treaty. There was more rioting and another assassination, that of the pro-British Sir Amin Osman Pasha in January 1946. Sidky Pasha, the Prime Minister, went to London and achieved a draft agreement with the Foreign Secretary, Ernest Bevin. It was thought in England that this would satisfy opinion in Egypt: all British forces would be withdrawn from Cairo, Alexandria, and the Delta by early spring of the succeeding year, 31 March 1947, terms which had already been agreed under the 1936 Treaty; but it was also agreed that evacuation of the Suez Canal and the whole of Egypt would be carried out by September 1949, provided that there was a Joint Board of Defence to plan against the eventuality of an attack on Egypt or on countries adjacent to Egypt. The joint defence idea was never liked, but the main opposition in Egypt concerned the clause about the Sudan, since it made clear that the Sudan was to prepare for self-government and to make her own choice as to whether she should be considered part of Egypt or not. King Faruk and all Egyptian politicians considered that Egypt had a right to sovereignty over the Sudan and, indeed, some argued that this was an even more important question than evacuation of Egypt by the British Army. This was a vital question to the landowners and farmers, as they did not want the British or an independent Sudan government to be in a position to control Egyptian supplies of water. Nokrashi Pasha became Prime Minister and took the question of the Sudan and of evacuation to the United Nations Security Council but without result for Egypt.

THE PALESTINE WAR

Events regarding Palestine suddenly moved quickly and Egypt was in no position to meet the emergency. The recommendations for the partition of Palestine between Arabs and Jews had been issued by the United Nations Commission in September 1947, and was approved by the General Assembly. The decision was opposed by the Arab countries who had formed themselves in March 1945 into the Arab League, of which Egypt was recognized as leader. In May 1948, the British government terminated the Mandate, the independent State of Israel was declared, and the Arabs were at war, the main forces being composed of the Egyptian Army and the Arab Legion of Transjordan. The Prime Minister and the higher ranks of the army were opposed to a formal war; 'there was nothing to be gained and much to be lost by demonstrating our military weakness', wrote Mohammed Neguib who recommended guerrilla operations,[99] but he fought gallantly and nearly died of his wounds. On the high ground twenty miles northeast of Gaza Gamal Abdel Nasser and other Egyptians fought obstinately in defence of Falluja, but the war was a disaster for the Arabs and allowed the Israel State to become established; an armistice agreement was signed on 24 February 1949.

The Egyptians had been led to expect a quick victory and were overwhelmed by the news of their defeat. The King, members of his family, and officials were accused of corruption in arms deals which had resulted in faulty equipment for the soldiers at the front. The Muslim Brothers' volunteers in Palestine had fought with determina-tion, and the movement gained thousands of supporters among peasants, students and military; the total was about two million. They were well organized and it seemed as if they intended to carry out a *coup d'état*, but the Prime Minister, Nokrashi, struck first by arresting their leader and sequestrating their property. On 28 December 1948 the members of the Muslim Brothers took their revenge by assassinating Nokrashi at the Ministry of Interior in the midst of the Egyptian police. Later Shaikh Hasan al-Banna was assassinated in a Cairo street. 'Egypt consisted of a hated King, hated government, and a sullen, docile people permeated by groups plot-ing in secret. The end was near. It only required the folly of the King and a new period of Wafd misrule to bring it about.'[100]

The British Ambassador patiently worked on draft agreements but the country was in no mood for any compromise solution. In October 1951, Mustapha Nahas, now Prime Minister, tabled decrees abrogating the Anglo-Egyptian Treaty of 1936, ending the Anglo-Egyptian Condominium over the Sudan, and proclaiming Faruk as King of Egypt and the Sudan; but this achieved nothing except to arouse further emotion, since British officials controlled the Sudan and a large British army remained on the Suez Canal. The Wafd maintained diplomatic relations with Britain but used the Muslim Brothers, who had declared a *jihad* ('holy war') against the British. Army supplies at Tell el-Kebir were stolen or blown up and British troops were shot at when maintaining communications to isolated places near the Canal; other organizations were used in this way, and the army arranged that the guerrillas should be trained and supplied with arms. Egyptian labour was withdrawn from the Canal Zone and there was a boycott of food and water supplies.

The Revolutionary Committee in the army continued to watch for the right moment to strike. Gamal Abdel Nasser took every opportunity to acquire information; he had cross-examined an Israeli officer, whom he had met during the Arab-Israel armistice meetings, on how they had organized their resistance movement against the British and had succeeded in mobilizing world opinion on their side. He sought some form of 'positive action', as he states in his *Philosophy of the Revolution*. In the early days of his political life he had believed that it was only through the assassination of those responsible for Egypt's condition that success could be achieved; he had considered the assassination of Faruk and some of his confederates – 'those evil geniuses'; he described how he took part in an attempted assassination and of the terrible night he spent wrestling with his conscience: 'Could the future of our country be really changed if we rid it of this or any other individual, or was it a deeper problem?' And the reply came out of the darkness 'It is a deeper problem'. The next morning he was relieved to read in the newspaper that the man they had tried to kill was recovering from the bullet wounds. He had decided then that assassination settled nothing. In 1950 Gamal Abdel Nasser was elected President of the Executive Committee of the Free Officers. But Nasser still remained very much in the background organizing the Revolt. 'It is a curious fact, and one which shows Nasser's extraordinary deftness and genius for intrigue, that his name should have remained unknown to the police till the very last day. He had strictly applied the basic principles of any secret society – that only one man must know everything and hold all the threads of the plot in his own hands.'[101] In autumn 1951 Nasser decided that there should be a trial of strength with the authorities at the November elections for the President of the influential Committee of the Officers' Club. The Free Officers canvassed for the election of General Mohammed Neguib against their enemy General Sirri Amir, who was the King's favourite. Neguib was elected and publicity was given to this rebuff to the King.

'BLACK SATURDAY'

Every day the situation became more tense; it was the British military authorities on the Canal who finally lit the fuse which exploded in Cairo. They wanted the auxiliary police to surrender to them in their headquarters at Ismailia and a badly handled situation resulted in the deaths of forty-three of them. The next day, 26 January 1952, rioting started in Cairo which the Wafd government was incapable of controlling. On that 'Black Saturday' much of the centre of Cairo was set on fire; nine people lost their lives in the British Turf Club and many British-owned buildings were destroyed.

The Wafd was discredited and during the next few months the country was in some confusion with various terrorist forces waiting for their opportunity. But the main battle was now in the open between the King's party and the Young Officers movement; it was a question as to which side would choose the most effective moment to strike. If the political police, which was a powerful body under Ibrahim Iman, had realized the part played by Nasser, that revolution would almost certainly have failed. As it was there were many complications and moments of high drama. When the Young Officers learned, on 20 July 1952, that the King was going to appoint their foe, General Sirri Amir, as Minister of War, they decided that the moment had come.

END OF THE MOHAMMED ALI DYNASTY

It was a bloodless *coup d'état* so well had the ground been prepared. As a senior officer to lead the movement, who would be known to the people, they chose Mohammed Neguib, who had been sympathetic to the movement but outside it; he was made Commander-in-Chief.

On the morning of 23 July Colonel Anwar al-Sadat broadcast news of the Revolution in the name of General Mohammed Neguib. The King and the government were spending the summer in Alexandria where the King had to agree to sign the document prepared for him and on Saturday, 26 July, Faruk boarded the yacht *Mahroussa* off Ras al-Tin. General Neguib went aboard with three of the Young Officers of the conspiracy, Ahmed Shawki, Husain al-Shafi, and Gamal Salem. 'Take care of the army,' said Faruk. 'It is now in good hands, Sire,' replied Neguib. 'What you have done to me,' said the ex-King bitterly, 'I was getting ready to have done to you.'[102]

NASSER AND NEGUIB

Egypt had for long been a sick country with the King, the landowners, and wealthy businessmen doing as they wished; democracy was only a façade.

For those who monopolized and dominated the means of livelihood of the peasants and workers could consequently monopolize their votes and dictate their will. The freedom to earn a living is a necessary guarantee to the freedom of voting. . . . Because of their increasing weakness, the revolutionary leadership which had championed the popular struggle surrendered before the mounting power of the palace. They all knelt down seeking the favours that would lead to the seats of power. All fell into the arms of the palace at one time and of imperialism at another. . . . Democracy on this basis was merely the dictatorship of reaction.[103]

That was President Nasser's report on the situation, and it is an exaggeration only in that he does not admit that there were good men working for reform but they were powerless. Fundamental changes were needed and so strong were the vested interests that they could not have been carried out without revolution.

What was meant by revolution? To Gamal Abdel Nasser it was not a military dictatorship 'to add one more experiment to the list of fascist experiments that had failed'; nor was it the work of one political party or group:

The value of a true revolution lies in its degree of popularity, in the extent to which it is an expression of the vast masses, in the extent to which it mobilizes their forces to rebuild the future, and also in the extent to which it enables these masses to impose their will on life.

But to many at first it seemed like a military dictatorship with jobs for the military and not for civilians. The military had to be rewarded and they were considered more trustworthy and obedient than the civilians who might try to reverse the Revolutionary trend. It was difficult, too, to find civilians prepared to carry out the ruthless reforms that the Free Officers intended to have, even though at first they did not know the mechanics of achieving their aims. They finally came to the conclusion that they would have to do it them-selves with the help of such able men as Gelil al-Emary, who dealt with Finance, and Mahmoud Fawzi, in charge of Foreign Affairs.

Gamal Abdel Nasser still remained in the background, although the prime mover; he was Chairman of the powerful Military Committee of nine which ruled Egypt but General Mohammed Neguib appeared publicly as the leader. This pipe-smoking General, friendly and charming, became so popular that he began to think that he really was the leader and expressed views in public which were contrary to those held by the Military Committee; this became known as the Revolutionary Command Council in September 1952. In the Provisional Constitution of February 1953, the Council had given Neguib supreme authority for three years which it soon realized was a mistake. Neguib made it clear that he was opposed, for instance, to the setting up of a Revolutionary Tribunal in September 1963, to try politicians and others of the old régime.

MUSLIM BROTHERS FIGHT FOR POWER

All political parties had been dissolved in 1953 except the Muslim Brothers, partly because it had powerful support in the army and throughout the country, and also because it had given a pledge not to interfere in politics. This cannot have been taken very seriously, for it was known that the Supreme Guidance Council of the organization considered that the Revolutionary Command Council had only carried out what the Muslim Brothers considered was their revolution. The Supreme Guide, Hasan al-Hudeiby, who had succeeded Shaikh Hasan al-Banna after his assassination in 1949, argued that the Muslim Brothers should supervise the Junta's decrees before they were issued. Since the Junta was working for a progressive secular State and the Muslim Brothers were working for a State whose Constitution was to be the Koran, it was clear that there would be a head-on collision. The Muslim Brothers intrigued on behalf of General Neguib and were endeavouring to destroy the government. Gamal Abdel Nasser treated the Muslim Brothers with circumspection because of their popularity, and also because the guerrilla battle against the British troops on the Canal continued and the Muslim Brothers' resistance groups were useful.

But by February 1954 the Brotherhood was taking such an active part in politics that it was banned. In the same month an Anglo-Egyptian agreement was reached over the Sudan which was to be allowed to determine her own independence or unity with Egypt. The differences with General Neguib had increased; in February he offered his resignation which was accepted by the Revolutionary Command Council, though, as a result of action by part of the army, Neguib returned later as President. The political parties and the Muslim Brothers believed they would win power. 'They all miscalculated because they were unaware of Nasser's character or capacity. During the next few weeks he showed his supreme ability as a tactician.'[104] The agreement over the Sudan was followed in July 1954, with the signature of a preliminary agreement to the treaty of evacuation of the Suez Canal, under certain conditions, an agreement which was bitterly attacked by the Muslim Brothers. On 26 October an attempt was made to assassinate Gamal Abdel Nasser at a big meeting in Alexandria.

The Muslim Brothers were regarded as responsible for this act of terrorism and nearly all the leaders were arrested and tried; six were hanged, the Supreme Guide was sentenced to life imprisonment, and others to various periods of imprisonment. The political organization of the Muslim Brothers was for the time being broken up, but the religious side of the movement, based on the Koran and against Western thought, still had a strong influence on students, young army officers, urban workers, and on the country people; branches of the organization remained active in various other Arab countries.

END OF BRITISH INFLUENCE

As for the British 'occupation' of Egypt it had come to an end with the Anglo-Egyptian Agreement of 1954 after seventy-two years, though since the Declaration of Independence in 1922 it could hardly be called an occupation, but the influence remained and had increased during the Second World War. It was this imperialism to which the Egyptians objected so strongly, 'an imperialism of interference without responsibility, which would neither create nor permit stable and orderly government'.[105] This influence was brought to a sudden and dramatic end with the Anglo-French attack on Port Said in October 1956, when the remains of the British base in

the Canal Zone, which it had been hoped could have been re-
activated in certain circumstances, was seized as part of 'war booty'
and British and French concerns throughout Egypt were sequestrated
and many were nationalized.

ANCIENT PROBLEMS REMAIN

The Free Officers were political descendants of Colonel Arabi.
General Neguib in one of his early speeches referred to the encounter
between Arabi and the Khedive Tawfik and quoted his remark 'we
are no longer slaves', and Nasser referred to Arabi, Shaikh Mohammed Abdu, Saad Zaghlul, and Lufti al-Sayyed as among the
builders of independence: 'the national struggle of any people,
generation after generation, resembles a structure rising one stone on
top of the other'.

Tawfik al-Hakim had written about the 1919 Revolution as being
'another miracle like that of the pyramids'. There was a new 'Worshipped One'; the first had been Arabi, the second Saad Zaghlul,
and the third was now Gamal Abdel Nasser. Egypt had had little
political education at the time of Arabi and he was faced by an
ebullient Europe; whereas by the 1950s Egyptians had acquired
more confidence and much had been learned. Europe had lost its
moral ascendancy as a result of events during two world wars, and
was fighting a stubborn rear-guard action to maintain influence in
the Middle East; the Port Said-Suez action of 1956 was an un-
expected, eccentric, and tragic death-rattle.

The Young Officers movement had worked on their Revolution
for seventeen years and had been successful, but they had no definite
plan as to what they were going to do for the country. Gamal
Abdel Nasser revealed very honestly the idealistic and romantic
streak which is part of the Arab inheritance:

Before 23 July, I imagined that the whole nation was on the alert.
I thought it only awaited the leaders to storm the strongholds of
oppression, to follow them in close orderly ranks on the Holy
March to the Great Goal.

I had imagined our role to be a commando advance-guard,

lasting only a few hours. . . . But the facts I faced after 23 July took me by surprise. . . . Every man we met sought nothing but the destruction of another man. And every idea we heard aimed at nothing but the demolition of another idea. Indeed, had we acted on all we heard we would have destroyed all men and demolished all ideas, being left with no alternative but to sit among dead men's bones and debris, crying over our misfortune and blaming our bad lot.[106]

He realized that he had expected too much; 'we live in a society not yet crystallized; it is still in a state of ferment and agitation'; the spirit of the thirteenth and twentieth centuries intermingled and inter-acted, 'a bewildering complexity tortured our minds and confusion destroyed our very existence'. But the masses, he considered, had shown that they wanted the Revolution.

Nasser agreed that Bonaparte's invasion of Egypt at the end of the eighteenth century had broken 'an iron curtain', opened up new horizons, and brought in new ideas. Egypt had been like a sick man in a closed room who needed a breath of air; 'instead, a raging hur-ricane assailed him, and fever began to devour his feeble body. This was exactly the case of our society. It was a dangerous case.' In these picturesque phrases Gamal Abdel Nasser described vividly the situation of Egypt. He found, too, as had other political leaders throughout the world, 'how easy it is to speak to people's instincts and how difficult to address their minds'. 'Never forget that when-ever you bring religion, or even superstition, into conflict with liberty, the former will always win over the latter in the people's mind', was Bonaparte's dictum.

Gamal Abdel Nasser continued the policy of secularizing the many functions of the State; but he warned Egyptians that while it was true that there were 'natural laws governing social action', that did not mean that they should 'accept ready-made theories and take them as an adequate substitute for national experience; the real solutions to the problems of one people cannot be imported from the experience of another'.[107] That had been the experience of the political leaders in the first half of the twentieth century. The other difficulty they had faced was the strong opposition of the religious leaders to secularization; this opposition Gamal Abdel Nasser had already experienced, in his battle with the Muslim Brothers. It is a battle for the allegiance of the masses. The Muslim Brothers gain their following through an appeal to the religious emotions of the people; Nasser has to show that he can improve their lot through Arab Socialism. In the National Charter the problem is dismissed perhaps too lightly and categorically:

> The essence of religious messages [and he includes others besides those of Islam] does not conflict with the facts of our life; the conflict arises only in certain situations as a result of attempts made by reactionary elements to exploit religion against its nature and spirit with a view to impeding progress.

One of Nasser's most remarkable achievements in this respect was to carry out a modernization of al-Azhar University; the very heart of orthodoxy. He continued the reforms that Shaikh Mohammed Abdu had started and introduced the teaching of the Sciences and also the education of women.

THE SIX PRINCIPLES

The government of the Revolution had six principles to guide it: destruction of imperialism, ending of feudalism, ending of monopoly and of the domination of capital over government, establishing social justice, building of a powerful national army, and setting up a sound democratic system. There were two main revolutions, one political, to recover the right to self-government which was achieved early on, and the other social – 'a class conflict that ultimately ends in realizing social justice for all inhabitants of the country'. For the first time an Egyptian government seemed determined to try to improve the lot of the Fellaheen and the first radical measure was to limit the amount of land which could be held by any one person to two hundred *feddans* (a *feddan* is a little over an acre). It is estimated that in 1952 nearly three-quarters of the cultivated land was in the hands of six per cent of the landowners. Expropriation started in October 1952 and has continued steadily since then; in July 1961 the amount that could be held was reduced to one hundred *feddans*; distribution to peasants was carried out more slowly than expro-priation. This discouraged landowners and encouraged the Fella-heen who are skilled and hard-working farmers; it is not the land that has been neglected but the cultivator. 'Egypt's human resources have been hardly tapped relatively to those not only of advanced, but even of comparatively backward countries.'[108] It is a paradox which Herodotus would have noted. As a result of their isolation the Egyptian labourer and cultivator had been cut off from develop-ments in education and health which permeated Europe for four hundred years. The numbers at school had doubled between 1933 and 1951 to nearly two million, but that was low in a population of twenty million. In 1950 it was estimated that seventy-five per cent of the Fellaheen suffered from the debilitating disease of bilharzia contracted in the water of the irrigation canals, while many suffered from eye diseases, hookworm, and malaria. Another problem facing the Revolutionary government was the high rate of increase in the population – nearly tenfold in the previous one hundred and fifty years which has made the cultivated area of Egypt one of the most thickly populated in the world.

From the beginning it was emphasized by Gamal Abdel Nasser and other members of the Revolutionary government that their main task was to help the people of Egypt improve their standard of living. Nasser argued that the 1919 Revolution had failed because the leaders had done nothing, or little, to help the masses and had left the power in the hands of the wealthy; it was that failure which led to the need for the 1952 Revolution.[109] There were, however, Egyp-tians and sympathizers outside Egypt who considered that Nasser repeated Zaghlul's error in not concerning himself enough with the problems of his own country. Zaghlul had had to fight for Egyptian independence; Nasser became involved in a battle for independence throughout the whole Arab world.

8   Arab unity and neutralism

IN THE PAST Egyptians had been more concerned with their own country and the unity of the Nile Valley than with Arab countries outside, but in the 1950s they considered it was necessary to co-operate with others in order to oppose the West. European civiliza-tion, which was at one time so much admired, had lost its magic; democracy, freedom, and justice had been 'betrayed' by the West in its dealings with the Middle East countries; nor had the Arabs any interest in the Cold War between the West and Russia; 'the title "Free World", pre-empted for itself by the Western bloc, rang hollow in Arab ears'. Palestine was the worst offence; the Balfour Declaration of 1917 was 'viewed by Arabs as not only an encroach-ment on Arab rights but also an act of betrayal by a wartime ally'.[110] It was the failure of the Arabs in the war against the Jews in Pales-tine which made Gamal Abdel Nasser decide that there had to be a new policy to prevent further encroachment by Western imperialism:

> I said to myself that since the region is one, with the same condi-tions, the same problems, the same future and the same enemy, no matter how different the masks he might wear to conceal his identity, why should our efforts be dissipated?

UNITY
The idea of Arab unity had long been discussed and dreamed of, especially in Syria; whereas in Egypt the approach to co-operation was practical, in Syria it was mystical. Some Arab leaders con-sidered that Arab unity had been there all the time, and had not been realized only because of the occupation by foreign Powers who

had set up barriers; these would disappear once independence had been achieved by all the Arab countries and there would be unity. They ignored, and therefore failed to deal with, the factors which stood in the way, such as Arab individualism, parochialism, and regional nationalism which had always existed, apart from any encouragement that had been given by the European Powers. Instead, they emphasized the elements which made for unity; firstly, the Arabic language shared by Christian as well as Muslim and spoken by over one hundred million people from the Atlantic to the Arab or Persian Gulf; secondly, the Arab civilization shared also by many Christians; thirdly, Islam which covers a very much wider area of the world than the Arabic language; fourthly, Arabic music, for Egyptian singers, such as Olm Kulthum and Abdul Wahab, or the Lebanese singer Fairuz are famous throughout the Arab world; the first two can charge up to four thousand pounds for a recital of two hours. From early days the Egyptian Revolutionary government laid great emphasis on the development of sound radio, which is a link between Arab countries, but each Arab country developed its own radio stations and in times of internal conflict the effect is divisive. The radio and the Press had to develop a 'middle Arabic'; while the majority throughout the Arab world understand classical Arabic of the Koran, it is not suitable for Press and broadcasts. A modified Arabic was therefore developed; in most countries it is understood, even though the spoken Arabic may be a local dialect.

From the beginning Nasser made it clear that Egypt intended to throw in its future with the other Arab countries: 'Ours is an Arab people and its destiny is tied to the destiny of the unity of the Arab Nation.' He blamed the leaders of the 1919 Revolution in Egypt because they had not extended their vision beyond Egypt and had failed to deduce from history 'that there is no conflict whatsoever between Egyptian patriotism and Arab nationalism'. History, indeed, had shown that there was conflict, unless, of course, Egypt dominated the proceedings, and that is probably what Nasser had in mind. Egypt certainly dominated the Arab League and lost interest when there was effective opposition.

In the 1950s in the Arab world there developed a debate between those who championed fundamental change and those who advocated the maintenance of the *status quo*, 'between *dynamic* and *static* views of national self-fulfilment'.[111] The division grew between the young radicals and the 'reactionary' monarchs or elder statesmen such as Nuri al-Sa'id of Iraq.

REGIONAL DEFENCE

Arab desire for unity, even though it might be only unity of aims, was growing in importance at a time when the United States and the Western Powers were determined to try to organize regional defence in the Middle East, as part of their 'containment' of Russia in the Cold War. Gamal Abdel Nasser, who was the acknowledged leader of those throughout the Arab world favouring what became known as 'dynamic nationalism', was determined that neither Egypt, nor any other Arab country, should become involved in the Cold War network of agreements; that, he believed, would mean the predominance of Western influence. It was considered that the Arab League's Treaty of Joint Defence which came into force in August 1952, established that all independent Arab countries were bound to observe the doctrine of non-involvement. Arabs did not consider that they had any reason to oppose Soviet Russia, whereas they had strong misgivings about Western policy. The Soviet government had taken account of the strength of feeling in the Arab world on such questions as nationalism and Arab unity and, after the death of Stalin in 1953, had begun to adopt a more sympathetic and understanding attitude to the Arabs. No reassessment, however, was made by the Western Powers, and Secretary of State Dulles waged verbal war against the concept of neutralism, while working to encourage pacts where he could in Asia.

THE BAGHDAD PACT

Iraq was ruled by the young King Faisal, his uncle Prince Abd al-Illah, and the Prime Minister, Nuri al-Sa'id Pasha; these leaders were much concerned about the dangers of communism in Iraq and the threat of Russia. Russia had for some time been exerting strong pressure on Iraq's neighbour, Iran, which had a frontier with Russia. The weakness of the Mussadeq government in the early 1950s made the Russian threat all the more real. Nuri Pasha, who underwent his military training in Turkey and had had experience outside the Arab world, was in favour of a Western alliance and did not resent European and American influence. In signing a Pact with Turkey in January 1955, he considered that he was following the right policy for the defence of Iraq. He was not disturbed that he was undermining the Arab League's Treaty of Joint Defence in which he had had little confidence. But to Nasser and other Arab nationalists it was considered as a betrayal. When Britain joined the Baghdad Pact on 4 April 1955, Arab nationalists considered it to be a striking example of imperialist infiltration and proved the correctness of Nasser's policy. He became the hero of Arab nationalism; his picture was displayed in cafés in Egypt, Syria, and Iraq, for there was a strong body of opinion which did not agree with Nuri's policy.

In England, Nasser was unpopular because of his anti-British propaganda over the radio in Arabic and in Swahili to East Africa. Sir Anthony Eden became Prime Minister the day after the Baghdad Pact was signed; it was favourably received by the House of Commons, but it has been pointed out that more attention should have been paid to certain factors:

> The age-old home truth that Egypt was the pivot of any Middle Eastern policy, the success Nasser had had in rallying the other Arab States against Nuri over Turkey, and the known reaction to new foreign pacts of the bulk of the Arab peoples.[112]

At the end of April, Nasser attended the Bandung Conference and found himself made welcome by such international figures as Pandit Nehru and Chou-en-lai, who also favoured the policy of neutralism. Nasser was much encouraged to find that the Arab nationalists were not fighting the battle in isolation.

PALESTINE

The next problem was Palestine where the situation was worsening. Arab refugees, many of whom could see their own land and farms

from the Gaza strip, had been infiltrating at night into Israel territory. The Israel government responded with military operations.
There was an outcry from the Egyptian Army, but the government
knew that it was not in a strong enough position to attack Israel;
instead saboteurs (*fedayeen*) were trained to enter Israel and destroy
installations. The Israel Army again responded with strong attacks;
that of 28 February 1955 was condemned by the United Nations
Security Council as a violation of the cease-fire provisions of the
Council's resolution of 15 July 1948. Nasser appealed to Britain
for more arms, but he did not consider that he got any satisfaction,
whereas he noted that Iraq received a large number of tanks under
the Baghdad Pact.

ARMS FROM CZECHOSLOVAKIA

In September 1955, he made the announcement that arms had been
purchased from Czechoslovakia; he did what Israel had done a
little over seven years previously. This development startled and
angered the West, while it was welcomed throughout the Arab
world and made Nasser still more of a hero to the Arabs. They
considered that he had struck a blow for independence and had
given them a new dignity and self-respect; he was described by
some as the new Saladin, who would reconquer Palestine. For the
West it was a serious interference with their plans. It was realized
that Czechoslovakia would not have sent arms without the agreement of the Soviet government, and they were alarmed at the
prospect of a new Soviet policy of giving help to the Arabs. The
Tripartite Agreement of 1950 between the United States, Britain,
and France provided for the control of arms to the area, though the
French government had agreed in secret to send arms and planes to
Israel; but now it meant that Egypt and the Arabs were in a strong
bargaining position to bid for arms from either side in the Cold
War, and perhaps obtain aid in this way as well. To the Arabs
this was known as 'positive' or 'dynamic neutralism'; to Dulles and
other Western leaders it was considered to be a dangerous bias
towards communism. On the other hand it was quite clear that
the Egyptian government did not intend to allow communists to

have any power in Egypt and there were many confined in desert areas. In his student days the communists had tried to persuade Nasser to join them but he saw then the danger, since communists were controlled by an outside Power and did what the Soviet government told them to do; that view he has retained. Whether Egyptians will always be successful in withstanding communist influence remains to be seen.

EGYPT AND SYRIA

Since it was considered that the Arab League Treaty of Joint Defence had been nullified by Iraq's action with regard to the Baghdad Pact, new arrangements were made. In October 1955, a Mutual Defence Pact was signed between Egypt and Syria, which contained the same clauses as the former Pan-Arab Treaty of Joint Defence, but omitted the economic section, which was dealt with in later agreements. The overthrow of President Shishakli in Syria at the beginning of 1954, had been helped from Baghdad. Abd al-Illah, who had been Regent of Iraq until May 1953, was intriguing to secure the Syrian 'throne'. Knowing of this danger, Syrian leaders turned for help to Egypt. Little was revealed of these plans to the British public at the time, though there were accusations in the French and Arab Press about British plots against Syria. 'We are witnessing manœuvres', wrote Le Monde on 21 April 1953, 'very probably inspired by Great Britain, to rouse Syria's Arab partners against her.'[113]

9   Renewed conflict with the West

AT THE BEGINNING OF 1956 President Nasser began to develop popular institutions and to obtain a constitutional basis for his rule. In January a Draft Constitution was published; a plebiscite was held on its terms and on Nasser's candidature for the Presidency. Both received a ninety-nine per cent favourable vote, and although Nasser was popular this was suspiciously high. A Cabinet was formed to replace the Revolutionary Command Council, and a National Union was to be established to take the place of all the political parties, but these developments were postponed owing to external crises.

President Nasser's government continued to rule autocratically, but that was in the tradition. Even reformers such as Mohammed Abdu and al-Afghani had been in favour of dictatorship rather than a sycophantic Assembly. There was anyway no doubt about Nasser's popularity in Egypt and in the Arab world. In the West he was regarded by many political leaders as an enemy; to France because he was helping the Algerians in their battles against the French; to the United States and Britain because he seemed to be on the Soviet side in the Cold War. There was an added reason for the British; they had for so long been accustomed to control Middle East leaders or send them into exile that they were non-plussed to find that Nasser refused to do what they wanted him to do and against him they had no redress. After the Anglo-Egyptian Agreement for the withdrawal of British troops from the Canal had been signed in 1954, relations had been friendly and Gamal Abdel Nasser had stated in August: 'after the Suez settlement there is nothing standing in the way of our good relations with the West'.

But there was no attempt to get on friendly terms by, for instance, inviting him to London. Britain cold-shouldered the nationalists and made friends with Nuri Pasha, who also discouraged contact with nationalists.

ARAB FRUSTRATIONS

The British liked Nuri Pasha; it was considered that he thought like a Western statesman, he seemed stable, and was 'un-Arab'. In fact, however, he was not a good adviser to the British government for he did not understand the deep emotions of the Arab world any more than the British did and he had a Turkish view of how to deal with Arabs. The Arab world was in ferment. Many of the thirteen Arab countries had only gained their independence within the previous twenty years. To some, independence was so recent that they still believed that the act of becoming independent would achieve miracles, others had had it long enough to make the younger generation disappointed and frustrated because their dreams were not realized. The West was no longer a guide to them, for they had lost confidence in what the West stood for. At the same time the Arab felt this alien presence everywhere around him; writers, archi-tects, technicians, scientists were all under Western influence. 'His ideas and ideologies, even of anti-Western revolt, derive ultimately from Western thought. His knowledge of his own history and cul-ture owes much to Western scholarship. . . . Even the gadgets and garments, the tools and amenities of his everyday life are symbols of bondage to an alien and dominant culture, which he hates and admires, imitates but cannot share. It is a deeply wounding, deeply humiliating experience.'[114]

Such was the mood among the younger generation in all Arab countries. Many had lost confidence in themselves and their Arab way of life, so that it was natural that they should look for a leader, who would show them the way to their own salvation, and reassure them that the West was not so important as it was made out to be. Nasser had the courage to refuse to be intimidated and had the strength to remain calm in moments of crisis. Like al-Afghani he did not believe that the British were as intelligent as people made out; he had written to a friend during the Second World War when British troops dominated Cairo, 'I believe the imperialists hold a weak one-trump hand – they are simply bullying.' At first anyway Nasser was practical and learned from experience. He did not himself create the high emotion of Arab nationalism, or the desire for unity, and the aversion to foreign influence, but he ably exploited and channelled the existing feelings. He developed and made full use of the Egyptian radio. It was a powerful weapon in encouraging trouble, but it would not have been effective if the national emotions had not already existed among the peoples concerned. When the British government sent the Templer Mission to Jordan in December 1955, to try to persuade the government of King Husayn to join the Baghdad Pact, there was rioting and trouble until it was announced that there would be no pacts with a foreign Power. Egypt was blamed because it was known that Nasser was violently opposed to it; that was to be expected and he had, he stated, been assured by the British government in April that no more Arab countries would be asked to join the Baghdad Pact. When in March 1956 King Husayn abruptly dismissed Glubb Pasha, the Officer Commanding the Arab Legion since 1939, it was once more thought that Cairo radio was responsible; it certainly had its effect but there were a number of purely Jordanian reasons why it was considered necessary that Glubb should go. President Nasser thought the British government had very wisely decided to withdraw Glubb and congratulated Mr Selwyn Lloyd, who was in Cairo at the time as Foreign Minister.[115] Presumably Mr Selwyn Lloyd thought it was a joke in very poor taste.

'THE PHILOSOPHY OF THE REVOLUTION'

Having started by not paying enough attention to Nasser, the British leaders and British people suddenly began to see his handiwork in everything that went wrong. The popular newspapers began to headline anti-British statements on Cairo radio which amazed, startled, and angered many an Englishman at breakfast. Sir Anthony Eden, the Prime Minister, recalled the Munich crisis of nearly twenty years earlier and began to think of Nasser as a little Arab

Hitler who must be stopped from increasing his influence. Western statesmen and officials began studying Nasser's booklet called *The Philosophy of the Revolution*, which was less than nineteen thousand words in length and consisted of a number of interesting but rather random thoughts. This booklet was given an unwarranted significance and was even described by Guy Mollet, the French Prime Minister, and others as a kind of Oriental *Mein Kampf*. It was regarded as proof that Nasser intended to set up an Arab Empire, and this was regarded as harmful to Western interests.

In the book Nasser referred to three circles which were significant to Egypt; the Arab circle, which was the most important, the African Continent circle, and the Islamic circle. There is a fanciful passage in which reference was made to Luigi Pirandello's play *Six Characters in Search of an Author*; it was stated that history was full of roles of glorious heroism for which no actors were available at decisive moments and that 'in this region there is a role wandering aimlessly about in search of an actor to play it'. It was considered, of course, that Nasser saw himself in this role, and memories were aroused of Mussolini and of Hitler; Nasser, it was argued, was showing signs of megalomania.

To the younger generation of Arabs the booklet was a factual account of the situation. They read nothing dramatic into it about conquering the Arab world. They wanted to get organized and they did not see that it had anything to do with Britain, or any other country, if they chose Gamal Abdel Nasser as their leader. It was not, in fact, the concern of the British, but they believed that they could still exert an influence in the Middle East; they had made friends with Nuri Pasha and with King Husayn of Jordan and they could not 'let down' their friends. The Middle East was becoming more and more divided between the young radical nationalists who wanted change and the older politicians who wanted stability and the *status quo*. Since Britain was involved, as a result of the Baghdad Pact, it was natural that she should be on the side of stability and the *status quo*. Besides it was necessary to make sure of the oil supplies from the Persian Gulf area and to help British trade which was developing in the Arab world. The methods employed were the ones that Britain believed to be effective. Military pacts may have been necessary at that period as a check to Russia but they should have been kept to the periphery of the Arab world – to Turkey, Pakistan, and Iran. The Soviet government watched the British government becoming more and more disliked because its policy was based on old methods.

THE HIGH DAM

Although Western politicians considered that they had every reason to be suspicious of Nasser, the United States and Britain wanted to maintain their ties with Egypt; they were prepared to help the Egyptian government build the costly High Dam near Aswan, a plan which had long been studied. The Egyptian government considered it essential to achieve greater control of the Nile waters so that the cultivated area could be extended and there could be more water released for agriculture in periods when the river was normally low. That was one way to deal with Egypt's rapidly increasing population, which had risen from under ten million in 1897 to well over twenty million by 1950. Winston Churchill had written about the first Aswan Dam project at the beginning of this century:

> And these gigantic enterprises may in their turn prove but the preliminaries of even mightier schemes, until at last nearly every drop of water which drains into the whole valley of the Nile . . . shall be equally and amicably divided among the river people, and the Nile itself, flowing for three thousand miles through smiling countries, shall perish gloriously and never reach the sea.[116]

At the beginning of 1956 it was confirmed that the World Bank would advance two hundred million dollars, the United States fiftyfive, and Britain fifteen million dollars. That was for the first stage of the dam's construction, and President Nasser was suspicious that there might be political pressure when he wanted to proceed with the further stages of construction; therefore he tried to obtain agreement to funds for the completion of the whole dam. That was refused, but the original offer was neither accepted nor rejected by Nasser. He may have already started feelers towards Soviet Russia;

during the previous year the Soviet bloc and China had been buying Egyptian cotton and there were other economic agreements: the most important, of course, had been the purchase of arms from Czecho﹣slovakia in September 1955. The American Congress was un﹣enthusiastic about granting aid to a country which was being drawn into the communist net, or so it seemed to many Congressmen; hostility was increased when Nasser recognized communist China in May 1956. Advised of this situation by the Egyptian Ambassador in Washington, Nasser decided to accept the original offer for the High Dam; but it was too late. Mr Dulles made a public announcement about the withdrawal of the United States' offer, which resulted in the World Bank and the British government also withdrawing. 'The High Dam was caught in the Cold War struggle.'[117]

Nasser regarded it, or pretended to regard it, as a slap in the face, and a punishment for his neutralism. On 26 July 1956 he reacted by announcing the nationalization of the French﹣administered Suez Canal Company and stated that the revenues would be used for financing the High Dam. In the Arab world Nasser became an even greater hero. The Egyptians considered that they had always been robbed of revenues from the Canal; they had agreed to pay compensation and there had been cases of nationalization in other parts of the world, so that they saw no reason why there should be such an uproar.

Sir Anthony Eden regarded Nasser's action as a further proof that he was a little Hitler. 'We all know', he said in a broadcast, 'that this is how Fascist governments behave and we all remember, only too well, what the cost can be in giving in to Fascism.' Mr Hugh Gaitskell, Leader of the Opposition, referred to Mussolini and Hitler, as did Guy Mollet, the French Premier. With Eden it had become also a personal quarrel – Nasser was not to be trusted, his record showed that – 'Our quarrel is not with Egypt – still less with the Arab world; it is with Colonel Nasser.' The British Prime Minister seemed to think that he could separate Nasser from the Egyptians and from the Arabs of other countries. He was determined to bring about his downfall. But in view of the circumstances the more Nasser was attacked the more of a hero he was bound to become. Sensible advice from Foreign Office officials, from British Ambassadors, from Eisenhower, Pandit Nehru, and others made no difference to Eden or the French. They had a complex about Munich, Hitler, and Nasser.

Because President Nasser and the Egyptian people kept their heads during the Suez crisis and because many of the anti-Nasserites rallied behind him, he was able to claim a victory, in spite of the failure to stop the rapid Israeli advance in Sinai. Both the British and French Prime Ministers had been intent on dethroning Nasser, but he remained and was more popular than ever. Nasser admitted that he had been worried at first about the reaction of the people to the bombing and the radio propaganda; but as he went through the streets to make a speech in al-Azhar Mosque after the Egyptian radio had been knocked out by the bombing, he had been relieved to find them all shouting: 'We will Fight.'

In the middle of October before the attack, President Nasser told Mr Tom Little that no compromise was possible since Sir Anthony Eden intended to attack him; he agreed that he could not hold out against Anglo-French forces and said, 'but I do not intend to fight them. I intend to stand back and wait for world opinion to save me.'[118] World opinion through the United Nations came to his aid, and also to the aid of the British and the French. To have held the Suez Canal or to have entered Cairo would have involved the British and French again in Egypt and it is difficult to see how they would have extricated themselves.

President Nasser claimed it as a victory against three nations, an exaggerated propagandist point, but there was some basis for it. M. Pineau, the French Foreign Minister at the time, has stated that if Israel had not decided to embark on the Sinai campaign, 'I am sure that the French government would not have decided to invade the Suez Canal'. It knew of the Israeli intentions, and at least some of the British Cabinet must have known. If the French government had not been eager to take action because of Nasser's help to the Algerians it is unlikely that the British would have undertaken the operation alone. The British bombed Egyptian airfields, which forced Russian Ilyushin planes to fly to Upper Egypt for safety and put some

Egyptian planes out of action on the airfields. If this had not been done the Egyptians would have been able to bomb Israeli towns and give air cover to the Egyptian troops in Sinai. General Moshe Dayan, the Israeli Commander-in-Chief, has stated in his published diaries that there could not have been the rapid advance of Israeli troops unprotected in Sinai if there had not been the British bombing; plans would have had to be altered. At the same time French planes were giving air cover to Israeli towns. Much has been revealed, but the whole story is not known. The terms are still secret of the Treaty signed between representatives of the French, British, and Israeli governments after the two-day meeting at Sèvres on 23 and 24 October; the Israelis attacked on 29 October.

To President Nasser the Suez attack was a gain, for it strengthened his position and it gave him some much-needed money. 'We were able after Suez to nationalize all the foreign assets in our country and by that Suez has gained back the wealth of the Egyptian people.' He stated that they prepared for development and for the raising of the standards of the Egyptian people. But did this happen? The Egyptians were getting a little tired of foreign adventures and wanted peace and a few benefits. What contact was there between the government and the people?

10   Union or not union

THE CONSTITUTION OF JANUARY 1956, had provided for a National Union, which replaced all the political parties and what had been known as the Liberation Rally; it was planned that the National Union would prepare for the election of a National Assembly in the autumn, but Suez intervened. Elections were held in July 1957, for three hundred and fifty seats; there were two thousand five hundred candidates, all carefully vetted by a National Executive Committee. The National Assembly served some useful purpose in enabling the people to express their views, but in March 1958 it was dissolved because of union with Syria.

The Egyptians had to wait, for Nasser was still involved in foreign affairs and Arab affairs. Suez had been followed by a Western economic boycott; the United States was much concerned by the increasing popularity of Russia in the Arab world. In January 1957, the United States issued what was known as the Eisenhower Doctrine, which proclaimed that international communism was a threat to the Middle East and that financial aid would be given to any government who opposed it. Secretary Dulles was particularly worried about Syria. At first it seemed to the Americans as if this policy might have some success, for there were a number of Arab governments, such as Jordan, Saudi Arabia, and Iraq which had been much shaken by the Suez episode and were nervous of Nasser's growing power. There was criticism at the time that the United States, like Britain, was backing the wrong men, and the suggestion that there was now a 'power vacuum' which would be filled by America was insulting to independent countries. Lebanon, Jordan, Iraq, and Saudi Arabia accepted the Eisenhower Doctrine; Syria rejected it and this strategically placed country became a battle-ground. The Nuri government in Iraq was trying to control Syria to prevent the spread of Egyptian influence there. On 23 November 1956, the Syrian government announced over the radio that a plot had been discovered instigated by the government of Nuri al-Sa'id in Iraq and at the beginning of the next year a trial opened. There was an Iraqi plan to invade Syria but whether it was more than a plan it is difficult to be sure. By the late summer, for a number of reasons, Syria was in a state of disintegration and the influence of Russia was increasing, though not to the extent that the US State Department seemed to think.

THE 'AMERICAN PLOT'

The publicity given to what was known as the 'American Plot' – the State Department was certainly being excessively active over Syria – embarrassed those countries which had given approval to the Eisenhower Doctrine.

> It was a little 'Suez' over again: they could not allow themselves to be found in the camp of Syria's enemies. . . . Washington, its gaze fixed on the Russian adversary, had tended once more to underrate the stresses and strains of the local background against which its greater contest was conducted. In short the net effect of America's brusque intervention in Arab affairs in 1957 was to confirm the Soviet Union and Egypt as Syria's twin protectors in the face of Western hostility.[119]

UNION WITH SYRIA

King Saud of Saudi Arabia had undertaken a mission to the countries concerned to try to isolate President Nasser and reduce Egyptian influence. The Egyptian President was not prepared to be challenged in this way; in October 1957 he landed troops in northern Syria to be ready to fight alongside the Syrian Army in the event of any move by Turkey or Iraq. He had made himself once more the champion of Arab rights and his action was welcomed in Syria. The move towards a merger between the two countries went forward and

178

on 1 February 1958, the two countries announced their agreement. The completeness of the union was prompted by Syria; President Nasser had misgivings, for it was not in line with his pragmatic policy, but as the leader of Arab nationalism he could not very well refuse the Syrian requests. The Egyptian view had been expressed in a book, published by Anwar al-Sadat in December 1957, called *Story of Arab Unity*; this argued that Arab countries should follow the lead of Egypt and no mention was made of any idea of political union. The plan for close union had long been enthusiastically preached by the Baath Pan-Arab movement, of which Michel Aflaq was the philosopher-spokesman:

We had the conviction that there could be no Arab unity without Egypt. This was not because we believed she was destined to be the Prussia of the Arab world, uniting it by force; nor because we thought that no other country could serve as a rallying centre. It was more because we had seen at work Egypt's powers of obstruction: she could and would successfully oppose any movement towards Arab unity which excluded her.

Another Baathist leader, Salah al-Din Bitar, stated:

The Arab idea never went very deep in Egypt; the ordinary Egyptian does not yet *feel* Arab. We, in the Baath, always hoped that a union would foster in Egypt the same nationalist sentiments [i.e. Arab nationalist sentiments] that fired us.[120]

It was clear that there was likely to be friction between the Baath Party and the Egyptians; both were working for Arab unity but on different lines; the Baath considered their policy to be democratic, and the Egyptian policy autocratic. The Syrians became restless, for they considered that they were treated by the Egyptians like junior partners and the Aleppo merchants objected to nationalization schemes. The union between the two countries lasted until the Syrian officers revolted in September 1961. To President Nasser it had been 'three and a half years of endless trouble'; at first he sent in troops to try to quell the revolt but wisely decided to withdraw them.

In the meantime there had been trouble in Iraq. Ever since the Israeli attack on Sinai and the Anglo-French invasion of Port Said and the Suez Canal, the popularity of the Royal House and of Nuri al-Sa'id was even lower than it had been before. They were being accused by nationalists of collusion with Israel over the attack on Egypt. On 14 July 1958 there was a revolution; young King Faisal, his uncle, and Nuri were assassinated, and Brigadier-General Abdul Karim al-Kassim took over power. At the same time there was a civil war in Lebanon. United States marines were sent into Lebanon and British troops to Jordan, but they soon withdrew without making any attempt to enter Iraq. The Hashemite Federation between Iraq and Jordan, which had been drawn up as a counter to Egypt, was brought to an end and King Husayn just managed to keep his throne.

It was thought by many at the time that Egyptian influence would now spread from Syria into Iraq, but General Abdul Karim al-Kassim showed that he was not prepared to lose Iraqi independence to Egypt and kept President Nasser at arm's length. The fact that the strong pro-Nasser element in Iraq had failed to bring off a *coup* in favour of Egypt, and the forced withdrawal of Egyptians from Syria, lowered President Nasser's prestige in the Arab world as the only leader. The Iraqis had their own nationalistic pride; the Syrians after the experience of Egyptian overlords for over three years decided that they had had enough. If, however, the United States or British governments had tried to force their way into Iraq, it is likely that Nasser would have been given another success.

After the overthrow of General Abdul Karim al-Kassim, who was shot with some of his associates in February 1963, there was a short-lived federation between Egypt, Syria, and Iraq in March 1963. It only lasted a few months, for the quarrel between President Nasser and the Baath Party continued. Since then no further attempt at unity has been effected, though Egypt continues to call itself the United Arab Republic with the idea, presumably, that sometime in the future there will be an organization which would include all Arabs, or, at any rate, all Socialist Arab countries.

53 The Revolutionary Command Council took over control of Egypt in July 1952 and ended the reign of the Mohammed Ali dynasty by exiling King Faruk. The Council are shown here: *front row l. to r.* are Gamal Abdel Nasser, General Mohammed Neguib and Abdul Hakim Amer.

54 (*left below*) King Faruk with Winston Churchill.

55 Mustapha Nahas Pasha who led the Wafd Party after the death of Saad Zaghlul in 1927.

56 General Mohammed Neguib acclaimed by the Egyptians as the first President of the Revolutionary Command Council in 1952. Nasser, the real leader, remained in the background but later took over control officially.

57 (*top*) John Foster Dulles, the US Secretary of State, between General Neguib and Colonel Nasser.

58 (*centre*) President Nasser and Antony Nutting sign the Anglo-Egyptian Agreement of 1954 for the removal of British troops from the Canal Zone.

59 (*right*) President Nasser and Sir Anthony Eden, the British Prime Minister, in friendly mood.

60 Friendship between Eden and Nasser was short-lived. Port Said after the Anglo-French attack of November 1956. This followed a series of quarrels culminating in the nationalization of the Suez Canal in 1956.

61 The Israelis had invaded Gaza and Sinai at the end of October 1956, but the operations were ended by agreement with a UN resolution calling for peace. A member of UN Emergency Force on the Gaza-Israeli frontier.

62 (*left above*) 'Gaza, Part of the Arab Nation' – a stamp issued in 1962.

63 (*right above*) Presidents Nasser of Egypt and Kuwatly of Syria sign the agreement setting up the United Arab Republic in 1958; it was dissolved three years later.

64 Despite the break with Syria, Nasser continued to try to bring the Arab countries together. Kings and presidents at the 1964 Arab Summit Conference in Cairo.

65 Folklore ballet has long been a tradition in Egypt. The Zacharia el-Hagawi troop.

66 The stick dance performed by the Reda troop.

67 (*top*) Cotton is Egypt's leading export. Sorting Egyptian cotton.

68 (*centre*) The manufacture of rubber tyres has become an important industry.

69 Egypt has produced textiles for several generations and the largest textile factory is at Mehella el Kubra shown here.

70 President Nasser was determined to build the High Dam at Aswan for industrial and agricultural development. Mr Khruschev attended the opening in 1964 for the first stage of the High Dam which Russia had made possible by financial loans and equipment.

71 The High Dam will form the vast 'Nasser Lake' which would have covered the great temple of Abu Simbel shown here being dismantled to be moved to higher ground; it has also necessitated the rehousing of thousands of Nubians.

11   Home affairs

ALTHOUGH PRESIDENT NASSER may not at first have expected a great deal from the political union with Syria, the attraction of it grew on him, for it gave Egypt a powerful position as it had done at earlier periods in her history. When the break came, therefore, it was a humiliating rebuff. In October 1961, the month after union had ended, he made a public statement that the failure had been due to *bourgeois* reactionaries who had infiltrated the Egypto-Syrian organization and also the National Union in Egypt. This made him determined to push forward with the idea of Arab Socialism.

From now on President Nasser's policy became more doctrinaire and inflexible both with regard to internal and to Arab and foreign affairs. He became more hostile to monarchical and feudal authorities in other Arab countries and decided that he could only co-operate with radical and Socialist elements, but he was wary of becoming involved in unstable Arab governments even if they were radical. He became more bitter against the West which had started a form of economic boycott.

NATIONALIZATIONS

In Egypt President Nasser carried on with wholesale nationalizations. After taking over British, French, and Belgian assets he turned his attention to nationalization and expropriation of Egyptian concerns. In February 1960, there was nationalization of the Misr Bank and the National Bank of Egypt. In July 1961, a series of Socialist measures were carried out to build a 'democratic, Socialist and co-operative society'; the working day was reduced from eight hours to seven, and it was decreed that twenty-five per cent of the profits of industrial and commercial concerns in both regions of the Egypto-Syrian Union should be used for employees in the form of social benefits. Four hundred private firms were nationalized in whole or in part and included banks, insurance, manufacturing, trading, shipping, and hotel companies. In December all foreign-owned agricultural land, consisting of about one hundred and forty thousand acres, was sequestrated for distribution to the peasants. The property of the wealthy Greek community was taken over, estimated as worth about one hundred and twenty million Egyptian pounds; in 1940 there had been one hundred and forty thousand Greeks in Egypt, by 1961 there were only forty thousand and they were leaving at the rate of five hundred a week and allowed to take only twenty pounds with them. That led to protests from the Greek government.

There were criticisms of these Socialist measures from Saudi Arabia and elsewhere in the Arab world. President Nasser attacked the rulers of the Yemen, Saudi Arabia, and of Jordan as reaction-aries arguing that conditions in their countries were contrary to the laws of justice and of God, and that Islam was a Socialist religion. He described the 1961 laws as 'the biggest triumph of the revolution-ary drive in the economic field'. The economist, Charles Issawi, considered them to be 'massive and ill-conceived nationalizations' which, with subsequent sequestrations, had led to a fall in efficiency and had discouraged initiative and savings. In the ten years since 1952 the country's economy had changed more fundamentally than at any time since Mohammed Ali. 'Egypt had become a totalitarian socialistic state'; ownership had been transferred to the government from the main branches of the economy, such as industry, finance, and foreign trade; rural and urban real estate remained in private hands though government control was tight. At the same time 'the successes registered by the military régime in its first ten years have undoubtedly been considerable – although they have hardly made a dent in Egypt's formidable economic problems', but there were heavy mortgages on the future; large foreign debts had been con-tracted and the servicing of them would be a burden for the future.[121] In April 1963, export cotton firms and ginning factories were nationalized as were another one hundred and seventy-seven companies in November.

The increase in centralization has led to an even greater amount of bureaucracy than there was before. It certainly worries President Nasser: 'Administration commits a grave error if it imagines its huge machinery to be an end in itself.' He was trying very hard in the early 1960s to improve the lot of the masses who had 'long been deprived'. 'The most important task that faces us today', he stated, 'is to reorganize the National Union to become a revolutionary instrument for the masses, who alone have a rightful interest in the revolutionary changes.' He wanted to make them understand what the government was trying to do and to bring them more into consultation.

During the period of the union with Syria some progress had been made in Egypt to encourage a system of local representation by the National Union, but there were so many changes that the people did not understand clearly what was intended. Elected executive committees were set up consisting of thirty members in the more populated areas and fewer in the villages; elections were held in November 1959, compulsory for all males and optional for women. Each committee, which came to be known as a basic committee, elected two men to represent it at the higher level of the district. In 1960 a law gave more power to local government exercised by twenty-four governorates; each had an executive council made up of officials of the central government in Cairo, of members of the National Union from the governorate concerned, and of two members of the basic committees.

THE NATIONAL CHARTER

On 25 November 1961, a Conference was held in Cairo to prepare for elections to a National Congress; this consisted of one thousand seven hundred and fifty members who were elected from labour, the professions, and the country districts. It met in May 1962 to hear President Nasser present a draft National Charter of about thirty thousand words, which he had drawn up himself. This was discussed on television, in the Press, and in the country districts:

It was the most genuine popular debate that the country had known. The National Congress discussions revealed the tremendous difficulties of creating a vital democratic system in Egypt. Nasser showed impatience as delegate after delegate stood up only to echo his words and praise him.[122]

Somehow Nasser had to vitalize the system and encourage the initiative of a people who had through thousands of years tended to leave everything to the government. In 1957 when opening the National Assembly he had said: 'To build factories is easy, to build hospitals and schools is possible, but to build a nation of men is a hard and difficult task'.

The National Charter has been described as Egypt's Magna Charta. It is certainly an important document full of wisdom and high ideals for the future, but can they all be carried out ? There are also passages of emotion about imperialism combined with Marxist sentiments. How England, for instance, robbed India and Egypt of their wealth, which enabled her to develop agriculture and industry. 'In their conception of history our people believe the States with a colonialist past, are, more than others, compelled to offer the nations aspiring to development, part of the national wealth they sapped when that wealth was a booty for all looters.' It is an argument which has received much publicity, but it could involve nations in difficult stocktaking. Was the development of cotton in Egypt which was bought for the Lancashire cotton-mills a disadvantage to Egypt 'leaving the Egyptian peasant starved' ? Did the armies of the Arab empires consider returning what they took from others ? Did the Egyptians think of returning the booty brought back from Syria by Thutmosis III to enrich the Temple of Amen-ra at Thebes ? Many such questions could be asked. In fact, the Western countries for the first time in history have shown that they consider the world as one and that those who are in difficulties should be helped.

How to deal with the main problems of Egypt and to try to help the people are the main concerns of President Nasser in his National Charter. One of the basic chapters deals with 'True Democracy' and lays down; firstly, that political democracy cannot be separated from social democracy – freedom of voting is valueless without freedom to earn a living; secondly, 'political democracy cannot exist under the domination of any one class, democracy means the domination and the sovereignty of the people – the entire people'. Thirdly, there was the Arab Socialist Union which had taken the place of the National Union and constituted the authority representing the people and the guardian of the values of true democracy. In the new Constitution there would be a set of guarantees such as organizations based on free and direct elections. In order to make sure that the farmers and workmen would have fair representation there is an interesting and important clause; they will get 'half the seats in political and popular organizations at all levels, including the House of Representatives, since they form the majority of the people'. It is also stated that 'the authority of the elected popular councils must always be consolidated and raised above the authority of the executive machinery of the State'. Fourthly, popular organizations such as co-operatives and trade unions should play an influential role in promoting sound democracy, and agricultural labour unions should be established.

CRITICISM

Number five in this list deals with criticism and self-criticism which are 'among the most important guarantees to freedom'. No one could take issue with that, but it is difficult to follow the logic of the argument about the Press. 'The ownership of the Press by the people', states President Nasser in his National Charter, 'was achieved, thanks to the law of Press organization [the Press was nationalized in June 1960] which, at the same time, ensured its independence of the administrative government machinery.' The Minister of Information and National Guidance, Colonel Hatem, stated in June 1964, to the National Assembly, that the government did not control the Press, but his audience also knew that if any journalist started to criticize the government in the way that a British or French journalist criticizes his own government, he might no longer have his job as a journalist. According to the National Charter, the freedom of the Press lies in this: 'The ownership of the Press by the Arab Socialist Union, which represents all the working forces of the people, delivered it from the influence of the one ruling class. . . . The decisive guarantee for the freedom of the Press lies in its belong-ing to the people.' That means no more than that the Arabs want Arab unity and therefore Arab unity exists. A British journalist working in Egypt comments:

> Criticism and abuse is now all directed abroad at foreign govern-ments and personalities who of course cannot answer back in any way which will reach Egyptian newspaper readers. Consequently Egyptian journalists can be as tendentious and inaccurate as they please in their reporting and comment on foreign affairs without fear of contradiction. In writing of home affairs, on the other hand, they find it difficult to avoid being pompous and dull. Most Egyptians have a fine nihilistic sense of humour which is still very much alive. Today it finds its outlet in a series of political jokes about the régime which, according to legend, President Nasser enjoys hearing during his brief moments of leisure.[123]

So-called ownership of the Press by the people does not produce interesting, lively, and effective newspapers. It is only the journalists who can do that and 'what the Egyptian Press lacks most is moral courage'. It is not easy, however, for anyone to have moral courage when there is so much talk of the dangers of being a deviationist; nor is it clearly defined what is meant, so that any form of criticism tends to be avoided and initiative suppressed. 'We do not allow any deviationists to remain among us', proclaimed President Nasser. 'Should a person deviate in any committee [of the Arab Socialist Union], this committee must speak up and seek to expel him.'[124] Previously Egyptians concentrated their talents on political writing; now they find expression in the theatre, television, films for the cinema, and in novels or plays. It is safer for intellectuals to express themselves in this way.

The need to increase production comes under the chapter entitled 'On the inevitability of the Socialist Solution'. The working day has been reduced to seven hours, but it is pointed out that there must also be 'a revolutionary change in labour duties'; labour, too, is enabled to participate in management and profits. Equality of opportunity, it is stated in the National Charter, should give basic rights to every citizen – to medical care, to education, to having a job which accords with his abilities, and to insurance against old age and sickness.

POPULATION EXPLOSION

There is concern, too, to improve the lot of women. There are now well over one million girls attending school, and family planning is being taught in the country districts and in the towns. It is stated that 'woman must be regarded as equal to man'. One of the main problems is the high birth-rate. Every year the population would increase by one million, stated President Nasser, and Egyptians must rely on their own work to produce more food; they would not sell their freedom to the United States or anyone else for wheat, rice, or maize; 'to curb the birth-rate is good for the family and for the country. . . . Of course, God provides sustenance, we know this and the Prophet Mohammed said they were to rely on God, but he did not tell his followers to rely on God and let the situation get out of hand. I don't want you to lose control of the birth-rate: we would then find we had lost control of the plan.'[125] By 1966 Cairo's population had increased to over four million and to help solve the problem of communications arrangements were made with the Soviet government to build an underground railway. The Prime Minister, Zakariya Muhieddin, who is Chairman of the Committee on Birth Control, stated that even with the completion of the High Dam 'the individual's share in agricultural land in 1975 will be less than his share at present'.[126]

There are, however, other agricultural developments such as the New Valley scheme linking the oases of Kharga, Dakhla, Farafra, Bahariya, and Siwa; these regions were fertile in earlier times and it is estimated that three hundred thousand acres can be irrigated in this way by tapping the underground water. Linked with this scheme there is another project, but it would be as expensive as building the High Dam; the plan would be to bring water from the Mediterranean into the Qattara Depression which is ten thousand square miles in extent and lies over a hundred feet below sea-level. It is estimated that enough power could be produced for a hydro-electric station to produce three thousand two hundred million kilowatts.

INDUSTRIALIZATION

It is in industrialization, rather than in an extension of agriculture, that lie Egypt's hopes for the future. Lake Nasser when full will cover an area of four thousand square kilometres and will store one hundred and thirty thousand million cubic metres of water. This great source of power will produce through the hydro-electric station, it is estimated, as much as ten thousand million kilowatts annually; there will be transformer stations at Aswan, Nag Hamadi, Minia, and Cairo, bringing power to every town and village in the Delta and throughout the country-side electrically driven pumps will replace the *shaduf* and the *saqia*.

The water of the lake can be retained or released when required throughout the year, so that there should not in future be any danger to crops and villages from a high flood; the many hundreds of watchmen engaged each year to safeguard the banks during flood time should no longer be needed. There is still the possibility, though a remote one, that the new lake may leak through subterranean channels under the mountains, and that evaporation under the summer heat may be higher than has been estimated. It has been stated that the High Dam will increase the national income by two hundred and fifty million Egyptian pounds each year, which would pay for the whole enterprise in about two years, but that seems a very optimistic estimate.[127]

UNESCO AND THE HIGH DAM

The High Dam, apart from the political trouble it caused, has roused world-wide interest because the vast lake will engulf hundreds of ancient Egyptian, Nubian, and Christian monuments. UNESCO and the Egyptian government played an important part in encouraging many countries in the world to carry out intensive excavations before it was too late. 'It is not easy to choose', said the Director-General of UNESCO in March 1960, 'between a heritage of the past and the present well-being of a people, living in need in the shadow of history's most splendid legacies; it is not easy to choose between temples and crops.' As a result of the great work done by UNESCO and by about twenty-four countries, the area, which is to be a lake, was intensively explored and recorded; 'in fact no large area of the world has been so thoroughly investigated by archaeologists'.[128] Besides that there was the dramatic decision to save the Abu Simbel colossi from being drowned by raising them to higher ground.

'This dam', stated President Nasser, 'has become the symbol of the will and determination of the people to fashion its life.' The really serious difficulty is the cost of the Revolution. There has been a great expansion in health services, education, and social services; wages have increased by nearly sixty per cent and there is considerable inflation. Savings are needed for investment for new projects but there has instead been a considerable increase in consumption of such commodities as cotton fabrics, cooking-oil, and tea; the cost of imports has increased, there is a deficit in the balance of payments, and loans have to be serviced and repaid.[129] It is a problem which faces Britain and other countries, but Egypt is in much greater difficulty for she has very little, if anything, in reserve. Are the people disciplined enough to face many years of austerity?

SCIENTISTS AND TECHNICIANS

If the bold plans for development can be carried out, Egypt may eventually become a new country. Egypt has for a long time been the main intellectual and educational centre of the Arab countries and for parts of Africa; students have come from all over the Muslim world and Egyptian teachers sent to many countries. A new and important development is the great attention paid to scientific and technical studies, especially since the Higher Council for Sciences was founded in 1956. There are many facilities for biology and technical research, electronic laboratories, an isotope centre, and an atomic reactor. Egyptians have long shown themselves efficient at running large concerns such as the great textile factory at Mehalla el Kubra; there has been a considerable development in light industry as well as the steelworks at Helwan. The efficient takeover of the Suez Canal surprised the world and it is considered to be run as efficiently, and probably less expensively, than it was run by the French; in 1955 the revenue was little more than thirty-two million Egyptian pounds; in 1961 it was nearly fifty-two million, and in 1965 it was eighty-five million. Of the two hundred and twenty pilots, one hundred and seventy-five are Egyptian. Improvements have been carried out by the Egyptian engineering firm of Arab contractors, Osman Ahmed Osman Ltd, and this firm has won a high reputation also by the work carried out at the High Dam in moving thirteen million cubic yards of rock. There were beforehand able bankers and entrepreneurs, but a new class is developing of scientists and technicians; together perhaps they will be able to save the economy of Egypt.

President Nasser in the National Charter refers to the responsibility of the universities and the scientific research centres for shaping the future; it is only with science that it is possible to realize the demands of the people. That includes atomic energy; 'we lagged behind in the age of steam and electricity. . . . We are now required, at the dawn of the atomic age to join those who have embarked on this age.' Without science, it is stated, popular authorities may inflame the enthusiasm of the people; 'no one has the right, at this stage, to deceive the masses with hopes. Revolutionary honesty necessitates that the masses should have a full picture of their responsibilities so that they may achieve their hopes.'

THE ARAB SOCIALIST UNION

That reintroduces the question how does the Egyptian government keep in touch with the masses; how does it explain what is being done and obtain from them the information required to make sure that the central government is planning on the right lines ? In the autumn of 1962 President Nasser stated that he was overworked and that it was a mistake to allow so much power and responsibility to rest on the shoulders of one man; there had to be a delegation of power. A Presidency Council was set up consisting of eleven members with Gamal Abdel Nasser as President; there was also an Executive Council, or Cabinet, consisting of twenty-five members,

198

under a Prime Minister, Aly Sabry; a woman was appointed as Minister in Charge of Social Affairs. The Arab Socialist Union was established in December to include all 'the popular forces' – peasants, workers, intellectuals, and 'nationalist capitalists'. There were about six thousand 'basic units' chosen in villages, towns, factories, large companies, universities, schools, and hospitals; delegates were elected to the district councils and then to the provincial and over all was the General National Congress of the Arab Socialist Union. Elections for the 'basic units' or committees were held in May 1963; and elections for a new National Assembly of three hundred and fifty members took place in March 1964, when one thousand seven hundred and forty-eight candidates stood for one hundred and seventy-five electoral districts; all had to be members of the Arab Socialist Union, which limited the numbers of the electorate, and half those elected had to be workers or small farmers. The Central Committee of the Arab Socialist Union had still not been established by July 1966.

PROVISIONAL CONSTITUTION

The provisional Constitution was published on 25 March 1964; the principal articles stated: the United Arab Republic was 'a democratic, Socialist State based on the alliance of the working powers of the people' (article 1); 'sovereignty is for the people' (article 2); 'Egyptians are equal before the law' (article 24); 'freedom of belief is absolute' (article 34); 'no law can be promulgated unless it is ratified by the National Assembly' (article 68), and 'the National Assembly has the right to withdraw its confidence from the government or from any members thereof' (article 84). The President of the Republic, in conjunction with the government, lays down the general policy of the State, and he appoints the Prime Minister and the other members of the government (articles 113 and 114). The President therefore retains considerable power; the National Assembly can get rid of governments and ministers, but it is difficult to see how it can initiate a new policy. Under the system of elections the people of Egypt, or at any rate a large part of them, are able to express their views, but how honestly they express them it is difficult to know, nor how much attention to their views will be paid by the Presidency Council. In March 1965, Nasser was elected President for another term of six years by a plebiscite. A new Cabinet was appointed with Sayyed Zakariya Muhieddin as Prime Minister; Aly Sabry, the former Prime Minister, became Secretary-General of the Arab Socialist Union. The permanent Constitution was being worked on by the National Assembly during 1966.

The sources of information received by the top hierarchy are several and could lead to confusion. Information goes to the President through the Arab Socialist Union, through the secret police, and there are letters from all over the country; there is the National Assembly and the Cabinet.

The President's drive, however, is needed to work the National Charter and the Constitution and to vitalize the whole elaborate system of government. Unfortunately, he is repeatedly deflected from home affairs because all Arabs are regarded as one nation so that imperialism can be combated wherever it may appear, and because the President considers that the Egyptian Socialist Revolution is for export; it was, he stated, 'for all Arabs and not for Egypt alone'.[130] He became once more involved in Arab affairs in September 1962, when Brigadier Abdullah al-Sallal led a revolt against the ruler of Yemen, Imam Badr. There was also discussion of federation with Syria and Iraq following the overthrow of General Kassim in February 1963; but it is the war in the Yemen which has occupied the Egyptians for the last four years. It has taken on the wider implications of a struggle between radical Arab nationalism and the forces of conservative and feudalistic Arabism, supported by the British, or so it seems to Arab nationalists.

12   Nasser's dilemma

WHAT IS PRESIDENT NASSER'S MAIN OBJECTIVE: to lead the revolution of Arab nationalism in the Arab world against the forces of 'reaction', or is he aiming to improve the condition of the Egyptian people? Does he think he can do both at the same time, and can he? He is in a dilemma which is to a great extent of his own creation.

As a result of Nasser's decision to support the Republican Revolution in the Yemen, sixty to seventy thousand Egyptian troops have been tied down there for several years and are likely to remain there for some time to come. In fighting the Yemeni Arabs they have had some training in mountain warfare, but Egypt has been in a less strong position to help other Arab countries to combat Israel, which has always been regarded as the principal enemy. The Yemeni adventure is, too, a severe drain on the Egyptian people at a time when they are being asked to lead an austere life. It is difficult to see how the fine ideals of the National Charter and of the Con-stitution are to be carried out, and how President Nasser will be able to convince his people that the promised improvements will be effected. The régime's enemy, the Muslim Brothers, would still seem to have an influence in the country; in August 1966, seven men of the banned organization were condemned to death and twenty-five others, including a woman, were sentenced to life imprisonment with hard labour; there were other sentences subsequently; in September the General Secretary of the Communist Party was sentenced to life imprisonment with hard labour and eight others were sentenced to lesser terms. The charges in all these cases were plotting to assassinate President Nasser and to overthrow the régime by force.

In pursuing the Revolution against feudalism and reaction in Egypt President Nasser's policy is in line with nineteenth-century Egyptian nationalism. He expanded this policy when he co-operated with other Arab countries to combat Western influence. Over the Yemen emotions have been aroused which are not dis-similar to the emotions aroused in the period before the Suez crisis. King Faisal of Saudi Arabia is seen by the Arab nationalists as Britain's new Nuri al-Sa'id, and the idea of an Islamic alliance as an attempt to have another Baghdad Pact. While the United States and other countries recognized the Yemeni Republic, the British government refused to do so, and seemed intent on maintaining its influence in the area as long as possible. To many in Britain Nasser is regarded as an enemy and some consider the British decision to withdraw from Aden and South Arabia by 1968 as a betrayal of the feudal rulers of South Arabia. Yet Arab nationalism and radicalism has been developing through many generations and what has emerged was predictable and, indeed, understandable.

There are those who argue that with regard to Arabia President Nasser is not prompted so much by Revolutionary ideals, as by a hard-headed ambition to obtain some control over the oil revenues of Saudi Arabia and of the Gulf, entering Aden when the British leave in 1968. This last is possible, but with regard to oil, it is un-likely that Egypt would be allowed any control by the countries concerned and Egypt is not in a strong enough position to carry out further warlike activities; President Nasser is shrewd enough to be aware of this. It would seem nearer the truth to argue that Nasser is driven on by his own Revolutionary ideals, and is caught up in a Revolution which he cannot, or does not wish to, control. Anwar al-Sadat in his *Revolt on the Nile* stated 'in every revolution there are two phases; first men lead the revolution; then the revolution leads the men'. That is what seems to be happening. 'Leaders have initiated social revolutions', writes Mr Charles Issawi, 'whose dynamics they are far from understanding and which will take them – or more probably their successors – to destinations whose existence they do not suspect.' It may be true that the large-scale nationaliza-tions, which have meant too much work for a suddenly expanded

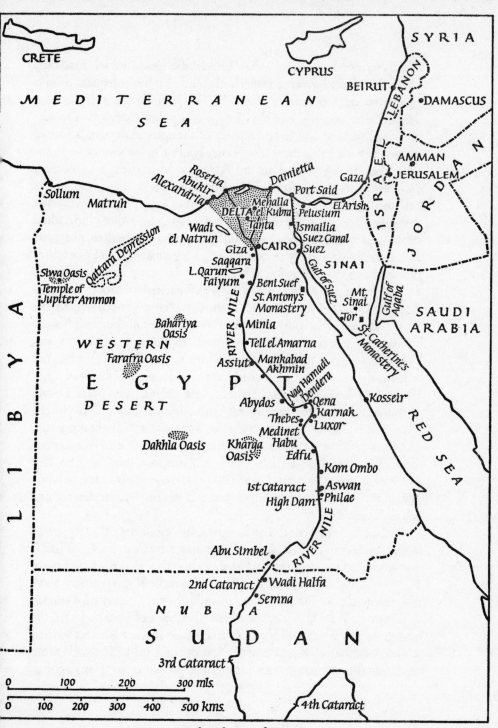

Political map of Egypt

and ill-trained bureaucracy, has 'broken the spring which made the old order work, however imperfectly' and that 'no adequate motive power has been put in its place'.[131] The periodic witch-hunts after deviationists and the fact that Egypt is a police-State tends to discourage initiative and independence of thought. After the failure of the union with Syria President Nasser became suspicious of reactionaries both in Egypt and in the Arab world outside, and became determined to hurry ahead with Arab Socialism. That may be the best method for Egypt; it was a question of catching up with other developed countries and that could not be left 'to desultory individual efforts motivated by private profit'. But what seemed to observers as a mistake was to try to introduce an Egyptian type of Socialism into other Arab countries, where it was in many cases unsuitable at that period, at a time when Egypt's financial situation was precarious. On 26 March 1964, President Nasser proclaimed to the new National Assembly that the Egyptian Revolution was 'for all Arabs and not for Egypt alone', and his subsequent actions and statements suggest that that remained his policy. In Egypt it has not helped the economy to banish the versatile and hard-working Greeks, Maltese, Cypriots, Italians, and others, who were mostly useful members of the community and added colour and liveliness. President Nasser is trying to revitalize what was a stagnant economy, but he is making people more conformist; this may lead to a depression of the spirit at a time when they are told they have to face austerity during the period of the second five-year plan. It is a battle which will be watched by many and it is not impossible that success could be attained.

Unlike a number of the other Arab countries, the Egyptian government under President Nasser has remained stable. This is partly due to his prestige and ability, but also to the geography of the country which has led to effective centralized government since Pharaonic times. There is today the advantage of a powerful broadcasting system and, as a result of the cheapness of transistor sets, the people of Egypt are avid listeners and aware of what goes on in their own country and in much of the rest of the world. Through radio the central government can inform the people of its plans and of what is required of them, though it has not made it any easier to find out what the people are thinking or what they want. There have certainly been important developments. Egypt has progressed as a secular State and the orthodox religious leaders seem to have accepted the situation, though the Muslim Brothers are still active; the old battle between reason and revelation, first started by al-Tahtawi, al-Afghani, and Mohammed Abdu, seems to be won. 'Only by eagerly welcoming the modern civilization can we have true peace of mind and a wholesome attitude to the realities of life', wrote Taha Husayn. That would seem to have been accepted, but not his recommendation to follow Descartes in a true scientific investigation of the truth of things. Egyptian writers still tend to make the past subservient to propaganda, so that it ceases to be history and there is much dangerous self-delusion. So suspicious have Egyptians become about Western intentions – not without some reason – that many tend to reject the spiritual side of Western civilization, arguing cynically that it is all make-believe. This may make them turn more to Russia, which has today great opportunities for accentuating the confusion in the Middle East if it wishes to pursue them.

At the same time by his determination and courage President Nasser has shown that it is possible to withstand Western political pressures, and by developing the policy of neutralism he has enabled Egypt to draw benefits from both East and West. In building his new society he has given Egyptians a new feeling of dignity and of self-confidence, and shown them that they can play a part in the affairs of Africa and of the world. The West is no longer regarded as an awe-inspiring and overwhelming force. Western ideas and institutions are being adapted to Egyptian conditions and there is no longer a legalistic view about constitutions. 'When we say that we must codify the Revolution', stated President Nasser, 'it does not mean freezing the Revolution. When we say we want to build the institutions and define their powers it does not mean stopping evolution.' It could be said that there has been too much evolution and not enough definition.

On the economic side Egyptians have shown themselves well

capable of dealing with big technical projects such as the High Dam and the Suez Canal and in September 1966, one of these very able engineer-technocrats, Sidqi Sulayman, was made Prime Minister. He had been Minister for the successful High Dam project and is likely to deal with the second five-year plan with bolder measures than his predecessor. Zakariya Muhieddin, the former Prime Minister, was trying to reduce inflation by restrictive policies and made some realistic speeches. Bold measures could be successful, but there are many risks. President Nasser stated, on 22 July 1966, that Egypt was spending more than she earned and importing more than she could afford, 'this is because we cannot wait'. President Nasser, with the aid of his government, has a gargantuan task and it needs all his vitality and talent to work the elaborate system he is building up; it requires, surely, a concentration on things Egyptian and a withdrawal from radical and Socialist adventures in the Arab world outside Egypt.

Egyptians blame 'imperialism' for most of their set-backs. Examples have been given in these pages of misguided policies pursued by the West to the detriment of the Arabs, but it would be a mistake to put all the blame on the West; other factors which have led to Egypt's difficulties should be taken into account. Many Egyptians, who are hospitable and charming in their own country, have adopted in Arab countries outside Egypt a patronizing and high-handed manner, inherited perhaps from the pharaohs, or caught from British officials, or because Egyptians have convinced themselves they have a mission to perform.

Then there is the Egyptian policy of revolution; it is so disruptive that it is bound to create strong opposition among other Arab States. Mohammed Hasanayn Haykal, the well-known Editor of *al-Ahram* newspaper and close confidante of President Nasser, wrote: 'As a State, Egypt deals with all Arab governments whatever their forms or systems. . . . As a revolution, Egypt should deal only with people.' It is justified by a remarkable piece of logic. 'This does not imply interference on our part in the affairs of others', continues Dr Haykal, 'since the fundamental premise of our struggle is that the Arab people are a single nation. . . . We have no right to separate ourselves from the struggle of other citizens of our nation.'[132] This doctrine would clearly arouse hostility in such countries as Saudi Arabia, Jordan and Tunisia. The West is not responsible in the first place for this division, but they become involved to some extent when these countries obtain arms from the West for their protection; perhaps it will not be long before they obtain arms also from Russia.

The failure of the union with Syria was a turning point in Nasser's policy. It is surprising that the Egyptian President and his colleagues, 'who had shown signs of distaste for the misty dogmatism of the Baath intellectuals, should now explain everything in equally abstract terms of a struggle between the forces of reaction and those of revolution in Arab society'.[133] This has led to the pursuit of a doctrinal unity which has resulted in the bombing, killing and execution of fellow Arabs in the Yemen and assassinations in South Arabia.

Then, too, there has been the discovery, already revealed in the history of other countries, that revolutionaries do not necessarily agree. When Kassim's revolutionary government came to power in July 1958, it was taken for granted by many Arabs that Iraq would automatically join the Egypto-Syrian Union formed in February of the same year, but that did not happen. Indeed, it was discovered that quarrels between revolutionary governments could be even more bitter than those with 'reactionary' governments, perhaps because 'radical militant organizations had a tendency to become prisoners of their own totalitarian ideologies and to see themselves as indispensable national saviours'.[134] The difficulties of achieving union are shown in the detailed account of the arguments, sometimes heated, between President Nasser and the Syrian delegates who came to Cairo in the spring of 1963. The discussion was published by the Egyptian government (its own version), and there is an interesting analysis of it by Malcolm Kerr in *The Arab Cold War, 1958–1964*; he describes it as 'a fascinating political document of first-class importance to all those interested in Arab affairs'.[135]

President Nasser stated, 'the concept of union is itself in crisis . . . political revolutions do not automatically entail a union. . . . We must therefore begin to look ahead into the future and draw the proper lesson from these events.' The lesson that President Nasser draws is not to concentrate attention on Egypt to make it a vigorous and prosperous country, which would be an example and perhaps help towards that unity for which Arabs yearn, but instead he plunges deeper into the jungle of the Arab magic circle. 'While every Arab country', he continues, 'boasts a party, union seems utterly impossible. True political opposition would degenerate into regionalism, with Syria at odds with Egypt, Iraq at odds with Syria, and so forth. For union to emerge, and for all immoral opportunist obstacles to be overcome, we must launch a unified Arab Nationalist Movement which would incorporate all the nationalist movements of the Arab world.'[136]

Notes on the text

INTRODUCTION

1 Mansfield, P., *Nasser's Egypt*, London, 1965, p. 212.
2 Ibid.
3 Nasser, G. A., *The Philosophy of the Revolution*.
4 Lewis, B., *The Middle East and the West*, London, 1963/4, p. 45.
5 Professor Constantine Zurayk of the American University of Beirut in an interview in a BBC television series on 'The Arab World', eighth programme, 6 April 1965, producer Maurice Harvey, devised by Gordon Waterfield.

I HERODOTUS AND THE ANCIENT EGYPTIANS

6 Warburton, E., *The Crescent and the Cross*, London, 1845.
7 See W. G. Waddell's edition of Herodotus, Book II, p. 139, and Edwards, I. E. S., *The Pyramids of Egypt*, London, 1965, p. 285.
8 Wilkinson, G., *Manners and Customs of the Ancient Egyptians*, London, 1837.
9 Dates for dynasties are taken from the newly revised edition of *The Cambridge Ancient History*, Cambridge, 1964–5.
10 *The Credibility of Herodotus' Account of Egypt in the Light of the Egyptian Monuments*, a lecture by Spiegelberg, Wilhelm, Oxford, 1927.
11 The quotations are from Gardiner, Sir A., *Egypt of the Pharaohs*, London, 1961.
12 The prosperous Greek city on the Canopic branch of the Nile southeast of what was to be Alexandria.
13 *The Cambridge Ancient History*, revised edition, vol. I, ch. III, 'Primitive Man in Egypt, Western Asia and Europe in Palaeolithic Times' by Garrod, D. A. S.; 'In Mesolithic Times' by Clark, J. G. D., Cambridge, 1965.
14 Madden, R. R., *Travels in Turkey, Egypt, Nubia and Palestine in 1824–27*, London, 1833.

15 Gardiner, Sir A., op. cit.

16 *The Cambridge Ancient History*, revised edition, vol. I, ch. IX (a), 'Pre-dynastic Egypt' by Baumgartel, Elise J., Cambridge, 1965.

17 Lacouture, J. and S., *Egypt in Transition*, London, 1958.

18 Note by Wilkinson, Sir Gardiner, to Chapter 37 in *History of Herodotus*, translated and edited by Rawlinson, George, London, 1862.

19 Legh, T., *Narrative of a Journey in Egypt and the Country Beyond the Cataracts*, London, 1816.

20 Quoted in Plutarch's *De Iside et Osiride*.

21 Wallis Budge, E. A. T., *A Short History of the Egyptian People*, London, 1914.

22 *The Cambridge Ancient History*, revised edition, vol. I, ch. XI, 'The Early Dynastic Period in Egypt' by Edwards, I. E. S., Cambridge, 1964.

23 Gardiner, Sir A., op. cit., p. 408.

24 The Pharaoh Djoser belonged to Dynasty III (*c.* 2686–2613 BC); Sneferu or Snofru, Cheops, Chephren, and Mycerinus belonged to Dynasty IV (*c.* 2613–2494 BC).

25 Flinders Petrie, W. M., *Social Life in Ancient Egypt*, London, 1921.

26 Carter, H., translation of *The Histories of Herodotus*, Oxford, 1962.

27 *The Cambridge Ancient History*, revised edition, vol. I, ch. IV, 'The Old Kingdom in Egypt' by Smith, W. Steven, Cambridge, 1965.

28 Safran, N., *Egypt in Search of Political Community*, Harvard, 1961, pp. 146–7.

29 Mosharrafa, M. M., *Cultural Survey of Modern Egypt*, London, 1947.

30 See Sayegh, F. A., *Arab Unity*, New York, 1958, p. 18.

2 ALEXANDRIA THE CAPITAL CITY

31 The quotations on these pages are from Forster, E. M., *Alexandria, a History and a Guide*, Alexandria, 1922.

32 Butcher, E. L., *The Story of the Church of Egypt*, London, 1897.

33 Muir, Sir W., *The Caliphate, its Rise, Decline and Fall*, revised edition, Edinburgh, 1924, p. 159.

3 ARAB INVASIONS

34 Butler, A. J., *The Arab Conquest of Egypt and the Last Thirty Years of the Roman Dominion*, Oxford, 1902. In this book and in Edward Gibbon's *History of the Decline and Fall of the Roman Empire*, the members of the Eastern Roman Empire of Byzantium or Constantinople are referred to

as Romans, but it is more correct and less confusing to refer to them as Greeks, since that was what most of them were.

35 Lewis, B., *The Arabs in History*, London, 1950.

36 See Russell, D., *Medieval Cairo*, London, 1962, p. 29, and Creswell, K. A. C., *A Short Account of Early Muslim Architecture*, London, 1958.

37 Russell, D., op cit., p. 103.

38 See Southern, R. W., *Western Views of Islam in the Middle Ages*, Harvard, 1962.

39 Lewis, B., *The Arabs in History*, London, 1950, Chapter X: 'The Impact of the West'.

40 Gibb, H. A. R., *Modern Trends in Islam*, Chicago, 1945.

4 EUROPEAN INTEREST IN EGYPT

41 Issawi, C., *Egypt in Revolution*, Oxford, 1963, p. 14.

42 Capper, J., *Observations on the Passage to India through Egypt*, London, 1783; Rooke, H., *Travels to the coast of Arabia Felix and from thence by the Red Sea and Egypt to Europe*, London, 1783; White, J., *Egyptiaca*, London, 1801. These quotations are given by a modern Egyptian writer, M. Anis, who points out how ignorant they were of the history of Egypt and of the Arabs in general. Anis, M., 'British Travellers' Impression of Egypt in the late 18th Century', *Bulletin of the Faculty of Arts*, vol. XIII, Fuad I University, 1951. He is now Professor of Contemporary History at Cairo University.

43 Carré, J. M., *Voyageurs et Écrivains Français en Égypte*, 2 vols, Cairo (Imprimerie de l'Institut Français d'archéologie orientale), 1932.

44 Hamilton, W. R., *Remarks on Several Parts of Turkey, Part I, Aegyptica, or some account of the Ancient and modern state of Egypt obtained in the Years 1801, 1802*, London, 1809, p. 330.

45 *Travels in Africa, Egypt and Syria*, London, 1806.

46 Volney, C. F. C., *Voyage en Égypte et en Syrie*, Paris, 1787.

47 Edward Lane had a very high opinion of him, and he has been described as 'one of the great historians of the Muslim world' (see Ayalon, D., 'The Historian Djabarti and his background', *Bulletin of the School of Oriental and African Studies*, vol. XXIII, Part 2, 1960). There are a number of quotations from al-Djabarti's history in Herold, J. C., *Bonaparte in Egypt*, London, 1963.

48 Denon, D. V., *Travels in Upper and Lower Egypt during the campaigns of General Bonaparte*, London, 1803.

49 Sonnini, C. S., *Travels in Upper and Lower Egypt*, London, 1806.

50 Madden, R. R., op. cit.

51 *Arabian Proverbs or the Manners and Customs of the Modern Egyptians*, first edition, London, 1830.

52 Burckhardt, J. L., *Travels in Nubia*, London, 1819.

53 Light, H., *Travels in Egypt, Nubia, Holy Land, etc., in the Year 1814*, London, 1818.

54 Legh, T., op. cit.

55 Turner, W., *Journal of a Tour in the Levant*, 3 vols, London, 1820.

56 The story of how he accomplished this difficult mission is told in his own narrative and in the excellent biography of Belzoni by Mayes, Stanley, *The Great Belzoni*, London, 1959. See also Belzoni, G. B., *Narrative of the Operations and Recent Discoveries within the Pyramids, Temples, Tombs and Excavations in Egypt and Nubia . . .*, London, 1820.

57 *Lettres écrites d'Egypte et de Nubie*, Paris, 1828–9.

58 Curzon, Hon. R., *Visits to Monasteries in the Levant*, London, 1849.

59 Madden, R. R., op. cit.

60 Russell, D., op. cit.

61 Lane, E., *The Thousand and One Nights*, London, 1838–40; a new and illustrated edition was published in 1865.

62 Burton, R. F., *First Footsteps in East Africa*, London, 1856.

63 Gordon, L. D., *Letters from Egypt, 1863–65*, London, 1865; *Last Letters from Egypt*, London, 1875; revised edition, London, 1902. Quotations are from these letters.

64 Creswell, K. A. C., *Muslim Architecture in Egypt*, 2 vols, London, 1952–9.

5 EUROPE'S IMPACT

65 Gibbon, E., *The History of the Decline and Fall of the Roman Empire*, Chapter 52.

66 Hottinger, A., *The Arabs, their History, Culture and Place in the Modern World*, London, 1963.

67 Gibb, H. A. R., *Modern Trends in Islam*, p. 19.

68 The extent of the influence of Islamic writers on the European Renaissance has only recently begun to be realized; 'it was not until the years between the two world wars that a serious effort was made to understand the contribution of Islam to the development of Western thought', Southern, R. W., op. cit.

69 Ahmed, J. A., *The Intellectual Origins of Egyptian Nationalism*, Oxford, 1960.

70 Hottinger, A., op. cit., Chapter 7.

71 Blunt, W. S., *The Secret History of the British Occupation of Egypt*, London, 1907.

72 *Egypt*, no. 1 (1905), p. 2; and Cromer, Sir Evelyn Baring, first Earl of, *Modern Egypt*, vol. 1, p. 334.

73 Young, G., *Egypt*, London, 1927.

74 Some of these are given in W.W. Blunt's Introduction to *Egypt's Ruin* by Rothstein, T., London, 1910.

75 *Pall Mall Gazette*, 1884.

76 Ahmed, J. A., op. cit., p. 37.

77 Adams, C. C., *Islam and Modernism in Egypt*, London, 1933, pp. 96 and 130–1.

78 Cromer, op. cit., vol. II, p. 134.

79 Gibb, H. A. R., *Modern Trends in Islam*, p. 123.

80 Cromer, op. cit., vol II, p. 154.

81 *Egypt*, no. 2 (1906), pp. 35–6.

82 Young, G., op. cit., p. 158.

83 Gibb, H. A. R., *Whither Islam?*, London, 1932, p. 63.

84 Reynolds-Ball, E. A., *Cairo Today*, London, 1907.

85 Landes, D. S., *Bankers and Pashas*, London, 1958, p. 323.

6 REASON VERSUS REVELATION

86 Hourani, A., *Arabic Thought in the Liberal Age 1789–1939*, Oxford, 1962, p. 190.

87 Husayn, T. (trs. Glazer, S.), *The Future of Culture in Egypt*, London, 1938.

88 Safran, N., op cit., p. 148.

89 Ibid., pp. 168–9.

90 A detailed analysis is given in ibid., pp. 169–74.

91 Gibb, H. A. R., *Modern Trends in Islam*.

92 Husayn, T., op. cit.

7 NASSER'S REVOLUTION

93 Others were Abdul Hakim Amer, who was to become Commander-in-Chief of Egyptian troops, Zakariya Muhieddin, who became Prime Minister, Gamal and Salah Salem, Abdul Latif al-Baghdadi, Husain al-Shafi, Hassan Ibrahim, Kamal al-Din Hussein, and Anwar al-Sadat.

94 Mansfield, P., op. cit., pp. 33–5.

95 Al-Sadat, A., *Revolt on the Nile*, with an Introduction by President Gamal Abdel Nasser, London, 1957.

96 See Little, T., *Egypt*, London, 1958.

97 Neguib, M., *Egypt's Destiny*, London, 1955.

98 Al-Sadat, A., op. cit.

99 Neguib, M., op. cit., Chapter 1: 'The Lost War'.

100 Little, T., op. cit., p. 179.

101 Lacouture, J. and S., op. cit.

102 Ibid., p. 159.

103 President Nasser's National Charter, May 1962.

104 Mansfield, P., op. cit.

105 Lewis, B., *The Middle East and the West*.

106 The quotations are from Gamal Abdel Nasser's *Philosophy of the Revolution*.

107 President Nasser's National Charter, May 1962.

108 By 1960, three hundred and eleven thousand *feddans* had been distributed leaving a balance of thirteen thousand *feddans*. Issawi, C., op. cit.

109 President Nasser's National Charter, May 1962.

8 ARAB UNITY AND NEUTRALISM

110 Sayegh, F. A. (ed.), *The Dynamics of Neutralism in the Arab World*, San Francisco, 1964, pp. 169, 172.

111 Sayegh, F. A., *Arab Unity*, New York, 1958, p. 161.

112 Monroe, E., *Britain's Moment in the Middle East, 1914–1956*, London, 1963, p. 184.
    On 25 March 1956, Gamal Abdel Nasser gave an interview to *The Observer* in which he stated; 'There was a brief honeymoon and then Britain plunged into the Baghdad Pact plan which she knew in advance was in our opinion a threat to our vital interests. It was also against the genuine desires of the Arabs. Any policy in this area must recognize nationalism. . . . I believe that by attempting to keep this area as a sphere of influence Britain will lose her real interests.'

113 Details of Iraqi activities with regard to Syria and the existence of an invasion plan were reported on during the Baghdad trials of prominent Iraqis. These had been ordered by General Abdul Karim al-Kassim's Revolutionary government in 1958 after the overthrow of the Royal House and the Nuri régime. See Seale, P., *The Struggle for Syria*, London, 1965, pp. 137 ff.

9 RENEWED CONFLICT WITH THE WEST

114 Lewis, B., *The Middle East and the West*, p. 135.

115 'Suez Ten Years After', No. 2, 'Egyptian Outlook', a series of radio programmes compiled and narrated by Peter Calvocoressi, in the BBC Third Programme, 7 July 1966, produced by A. Moncrieff.

116 Churchill, W., *The River War*, London, 1899.

117 Little, T., *High Dam at Aswan*, London, 1965.

118 'Suez Ten Years After', No. 2, 'Egyptian Outlook', BBC Third Programme, 7 July 1966. Reference is also made subsequently to No. 3, 'Israel and the Middle East', broadcast 14 July 1966, for the statement by M. Pineau.

10 UNION OR NOT UNION

119 Seale, P., op. cit., pp. 302-3.

120 Ibid., pp. 310-11.

11 HOME AFFAIRS

121 Issawi, C., op. cit., pp. 46-8.

122 Mansfield, P., op. cit., p. 197.

123 Ibid., p. 127.

124 Speech by President Nasser, 22 July 1966.

125 Ibid.

126 Statement by al-Sayyed Zakariya Muhieddin before the National Assembly, Cairo, 4 December 1965.

127 Little, T., *High Dam at Aswan*, London, 1965.

128 Emery, W. B., *Egypt in Nubia*, London, 1965, Chapter 5: 'The Results of the Unesco Appeal'.

129 See statement by the Prime Minister, al-Sayyed Zakariya Muhieddin, before the National Assembly, Cairo, 4 December 1965.

130 Statement to the National Assembly, 26 March 1964.

12 NASSER'S DILEMMA

131 Issawi, C., op. cit.

132 Haykal, M. H., *al-Ahram*, 29 December 1962.

133 Kerr, M., *The Arab Cold War, 1958-1964*, Oxford, 1965, pp. 33-4.

134 Ibid., p. 120.

135 Ibid., p. 63; see also President Nasser's speech violently attacking the Baath Party, 22 July 1963; *Speeches and Press Interviews*, Cairo, 1963, pp. 118ff.

136 *Arab Political Documents, 1963* (American University of Beirut), p. 333, quoted in Kerr, M., *The Arab Cold War*, pp. 119-20.

Select Bibliography

CHAPTER I

The Cambridge Ancient History, revised edition, Cambridge, 1964–5
Gardiner, Sir A., Egypt of the Pharaohs, London, 1961
Edwards, I. E. S., The Pyramids of Egypt, London, 1965
Carter, H., The Histories of Herodotus of Halicarnassus, Book II, Euterpe, Oxford, 1962
Hurst, H. E., The Nile, London, 1952

CHAPTER 2

Forster, E. M., Alexandria, a History and a Guide, Alexandria, 1922; New York, 1961
Gibbon, E., The History of the Decline and Fall of the Roman Empire, 1776–8
Butcher, E. L., The Story of the Church of Egypt, London, 1897

CHAPTER 3

Butler, A. J., The Arab Conquest of Egypt and the Last Thirty Years of the Roman Dominion, Oxford, 1902
Muir, Sir W., The Caliphate, its Rise, Decline and Fall, revised edition, Edinburgh, 1924
Lewis, B., The Arabs in History, London, 1950
Hottinger, A., The Arabs, their History, Culture and Place in the Modern World, London, 1963
Russell, D., Medieval Cairo, London, 1962
Creswell, K. A. C., A Short Account of Early Muslim Architecture, London, 1958

CHAPTER 4

Herold, J. C., Bonaparte in Egypt, London, 1963
Mayes, Stanley, The Great Belzoni, London, 1959

Lane, Edward, *Manners and Customs of the Modern Egyptians*, London, 1836

Waterfield, Gordon, *Lucie Duff Gordon*, London, 1937

Kinglake, A. W., *Eothen*, London, 1844

CHAPTERS 5–12

Hourani, A., *Arabic Thought in the Liberal Age, 1798–1939*, Oxford, 1962

Gibb, H. A. R., *Modern Trends in Islam*, Chicago, 1945; *Whither Islam?*, London, 1932

Elgood, P. G., *The Transit of Egypt*, London, 1928

Lacouture, J. and S., *Egypt in Transition*, London, 1958

Little, T., *Egypt*, London, 1958; *High Dam at Aswan*, London, 1965

Young, G., *Egypt*, London, 1927

Monroe, E., *Britain's Moment in the Middle East, 1914–1956*, London, 1963

Ahmed, J. M., *The Intellectual Origins of Egyptian Nationalism*, Oxford, 1960.

Kirk, G., *The Middle East, 1945–1950*, London, 1954

Seale, P., *The Struggle for Syria*, Oxford, 1965

Issawi, C., *Egypt in Revolution*, Oxford, 1963

Mansfield, P., *Nasser's Egypt*, London, 1965

Lewis, B., *The Middle East and the West*, London, 1963–4

Marlowe, J., *Four Aspects of Egypt*, London, 1966

Kerr, M., *The Arab Cold War, 1958–1964*, Oxford, 1965

Berque, J., *The Arabs, Their History and Future*, London, 1964

Safran, N., *Egypt in Search of Political Community*, Harvard, 1961

Sayegh, F. A., *Arab Unity*, New York, 1958; *The Dynamics of Neutralism in the Arab World*, San Francisco, 1964

Nasser, President G. A., *Speeches and Press Interviews*, Cairo, 1963

Who's Who

ABDU, Shaikh Mohammed (1849–1905). A great religious reformer, whose teachings still exert an influence today. He was exiled from Egypt for his part in the nationalist revolt against the Khedive Tawfik, but returned to Egypt and became Grand Mufti in 1899.

AFGHANI, Jamal al-Din al- (1839–97). Revolutionary reformer of Islam; travelled in India, the Ottoman Empire, and Europe. He spent seven years in Egypt and helped to inspire the national revolt of Ahmed Arabi.

ALEXANDER, the Great (356–323 BC). King of Macedonia, educated by Aristotle, conquered the Persian Empire which included Egypt, and founded the city of Alexandria; but he died before seeing it at the age of thirty-three after returning to Babylon in Mesopotamia following his expedition to India.

ALLENBY, Lord (1861–1936). Commanded the British forces in the Middle East (1917–19), promoted to Field-Marshal; he was British High Commissioner in Egypt from 1919 to 1925 and was responsible for the Declaration of Independence of 1922.

AMER, Abdul Hakim (b. 1900). Close friend of Nasser, member of the original Council of the Revolution, became Minister of War and Assistant Commander-in-Chief of the Egyptian Army.

AMR, Ibn al-A s (c. 573–663). Converted to Islam in middle age, and conquered Egypt by the autumn of AD 642 – a man of moderation with considerable political talent, and a great military leader.

ARABI, Ahmed (also spelt Urabi) (1839–1911). Rose to Colonel in the Egyptian Army and was Minister of War under Khedive Tawfik; he led a

218

revolt against the Khedive and was defeated by the British Army at the Battle of Tell el-Kebir in 1882. Exiled to Ceylon but returned to Cairo at the beginning of the century.

BONAPARTE, Napoleon I (1769–1821). Landed in Egypt in 1798 with his army where he was cut off following the defeat of his fleet by Nelson at the Battle of the Nile; he returned to France in 1799, becoming First Consul and virtual Dictator.

BELZONI, Giovanni Battista (1778–1823). Was six foot seven inches in height and carried out feats of strength at fairs in England. He went to Egypt in 1815 with an invention for raising Nile water, but turned to archaeological discovery and became famous. He died in West Africa trying to reach Timbuktu.

BURCKHARDT, John Lewis (1784–1817). Swiss traveller and Orientalist, visited Mecca and wrote of his travels in Arabia and Nubia. He was planning to go with a Muslim caravan across Africa from Cairo to try to reach Timbuktu, but died in Cairo of dysentery before departure.

CHAMPOLLION, Jean-François (1790–1832). French Egyptologist, who won the race to decipher hieroglyphs.

CROMER, Lord (Evelyn Baring) (1841–1917). British Consul-General in Egypt and virtual ruler of the country from 1883 to 1907.

DJABARTI, al- (or al-Jabarti), Shaikh abd al-Rahman (1754–1822). He is famous for his history of the period of the French occupation and of the early part of the reign of Mohammed Ali, who, it is believed, had him murdered when he learned of the views he had expressed.

DULLES, John Foster (1888–1959). He visited Egypt in 1953 after becoming President Eisenhower's Secretary of State.

EDEN, Sir Anthony (Lord Avon) (b. 1897). In 1935 he became Foreign Secretary, but resigned in 1938 because he objected to the British government opening conversations with Mussolini; he became Foreign Secretary, 1940–5, returned to the Foreign Office in 1951, and then succeeded Winston Churchill as Prime Minister; he resigned after the Anglo-French landing at Port Said in October 1956.

FARUK, King of Egypt (1920–65). He succeeded his father, Fuad I, in 1936 and was forced to abdicate in 1952 as a result of the military revolution led by Nasser and Neguib.

FUAD I, Ahmed (1868–1936). King of Egypt after the Declaration of Independence in 1922. He was a son of Khedive Ismail and accompanied him abroad when he was exiled in 1879. As king he patronized historical studies and encouraged education.

HAYKAL, Mohammed Husayn (1889–1956). Author; leader of the Liberal Party and President of the Egyptian Senate.

HERODOTUS (484–424 BC). Widely travelled Greek historian who mostly interested himself in the manners and customs of various races which he described in his great work on the epic struggle between Greece and Persia. He visited Egypt from August to November c. 450 BC or a little later, and describes the people and the country in Book II of his history.

HUSAYN, Taha (b. 1889). Born of a poor family in Upper Egypt, has been blind since the age of three. He has exerted great influence by his writings as a philosopher and reformer, much influenced by the learning of Europe and opposed to the orthodox religious leaders who have been against reform.

KAMIL, Mustapha (1874–1908). National leader, had great influence as an orator and wrote in favour of independence for Egypt in the French Press.

KITCHENER, H. H., Earl Kitchener of Khartum (1850–1916). Began service in the Egyptian Army in 1882 and became Commander-in-Chief in 1892; he reoccupied Khartum in 1898 and planned the streets in the form of a Union Jack. Kitchener was British Agent in Egypt in 1914 and then was appointed Minister for War in the British government after the outbreak of the First World War.

LANE, Edward W. (1801–76). Author and Orientalist, visited Egypt from 1825 to 1828 and from 1833 to 1835, publishing his famous work *Manners and Customs of the Modern Egyptians* in 1836 and a translation of *The Thousand and One Nights* (*The Arabian Nights*), 1838–40.

MOHAMMED ALI (1769–1848). Ruler of Egypt, born at Cavalla in Greece then part of the Ottoman Empire, member of the Albanian detachment of the Turkish forces which landed at Abukir in 1799 and were defeated by the French under Bonaparte; elected Viceroy of Egypt by the Shaikhs and notables in May 1805, and confirmed as ruler by the Sultan of Turkey. He proclaimed his ownership of the soil of Egypt, tried to industrialize the country, and conscripted the peasants to fight in the armies of his son Ibrahim who defeated the Turkish forces.

MUHIEDDIN, Zakariya (b. 1918). Member of the Council of the Revolution in 1952, became Minister of the Interior and later Prime Minister.

NASSER, Gamal Abdel, President of the United Arab Republic, b. 15 January 1918, at Beni Mer in Assiut Province, son of a postal clerk; he was the eldest of three brothers and his mother died when he was eight years old. He joined the Military Academy in 1937 and was posted to Mankabad near Assiut; served in Alexandria, Alamein area, and in the Sudan (two years). In 1942 he went to the General Staff College, married 1944, has five children. He was wounded during the war in Palestine helping to defend the Falluja pocket; founded the Free Officers organization; lecturer at the General Staff College; planned and led the Revolution of 23 July 1952, when King Faruk was exiled and the Republic of Egypt established; elected President, June 1956.

NEGUIB, General Mohammed (b. 1901). Fought in the war in Palestine in 1948 and was severely wounded. Chosen as the figure-head of the military revolution of 1952, appointed Prime Minister in September 1952, and later President of the Republic; resigned March 1954 and was put under house arrest from which he was released later.

SADAT, Anwar al- (b. 1918). Member of Nasser's Council of the Revolution, became Minister of State, but left the government in June 1956 and became Managing Editor of the daily newspaper, al-Goumhouriya. Author of Revolt on the Nile.

SA'ID Pasha, Nuri al- (1888–1958). Trained in the Turkish Army, fought on the side of Arab independence in the First World War, many years Prime Minister of Iraq, assassinated with King Faisal II and his uncle Prince Abd al-Illah during revolt of Brigadier-General Abdul Karim al-Kassim in 1958.

SALADIN, Salah al-Din Yusuf ibn Ayyub (1138–93). Son of Amir Nadjm al-Din Ayyub. He was a Kurd born at Takrit on the Tigris and was a patron of scholars and of theological learning, and had carried out a number of important buildings in Cairo and in Jerusalem. He conquered Egypt in 1164 and Syria 1174–87; Saladin recovered Jerusalem from the Christian Crusaders in 1187 and repelled the attacks of Richard I of England in 1192 when peace was concluded for a time.

ZAGHLUL, Saad (1860–1927). Egyptian nationalist leader, deported by the British first to Malta and then to the Seychelles; he became Prime Minister of Egypt in 1924.

Acknowledgements

By kind permission of Miss A. al-Sayyed, 51; Arthaud, 1; Associated Press Ltd, 70; British Broadcasting Corporation, 52; from J. L. Burchardt, *Travels in Nubia*, London, 1819, 28; Camera Press Ltd, 3, 67; photo: P. Clayton, 17; by kind permission of the Director, Service des Antiquities, Cairo Museum, 7, 8, 13, 14; from *Description de l'Egypte*, Paris, 1821, photo: John R. Freeman, 20, 25, 31, 32, 33, 34; Egypt Exploration Fund, 11; photo: Hachette, 24; *Illustrated London News*, 39; A. Jänicke, 9; A. R. Kersting, 21; Keystone Press Agency, 53, 56, 57, 58, 59, 69, 61, 63, 64; Max Hirmer, 6, 10; The Metropolitan Museum of Art, New York. Bequest of Mrs H. O. Havemayer, 1929, The H. O. Havemeyer Collection, 12; The Mansell Collection, 15, 26, 37, 42, 44, 45, 47, 48, 49; by kind permission of John Murray Ltd, 36; Oriental Institute, University of Chicago, 2; from R. Pocock, *Description of the East*, London, 1743, 19; M. Rowlatt, 18, 38, 54; Radio Times Hulton Picture Library, 43, 45, 50, 55; Stanley Gibbons Ltd, 62; by kind permission of the Trustees of the British Museum, 16; UNESCO, 71; United Arab Republic Tourist and Information Centre, 65, 66, 68, 69; by kind permission of the owners Major and Mrs Alec Wise, 4.

Index

Cromer on, 111; defeated and tried, 113

Arab League, the, formed, 152; Egypt dominates, 164; Treaty of Joint Defence, 165, 168; Nuri Pasha undermines Treaty, 166

Aristarchus of Samos, 36

Arius, and the nature of Christ, 41

Aswan, 13, 75; Nilometer at, 18; the Dam, 18, 120

Augustus, Octavian, 38

Azhar, al-, the Mosque at, 58, 175; Ulama of, 126-7; University, 128, 129, 161.

BABYLON (Egypt), besieged by Arab army, 53; captured, 54

Babylon (Mesopotamia), Alexander the Great dies at, 35

Baghdad, 56; Muslim thought in, 58; captured by Turks, 59

Baghdad Pact, the, 166, 167, 168, 172

Banks, Sir Joseph, 75, 78

Banna, Hasan al-, founds Muslim Brothers, 149-51; assassinated, 153

Baring, Evelyn, see Cromer, Lord

Belzoni, Giovanni (see Who's Who, p. 219), 29, and Burckhardt, 77; and the 'Memnon', 78; dines with troglodytes, 79; and the Cleopatra obelisk, 80

Benjamin, Patriarch, 44, 55

Bevin, Ernest, drafts agreement with Egypt, 151

Bey, Murad, 71, 25

Blunt, Wilfrid Scawen, and Ahmed Arabi, 110, 111

Bonaparte, Napoleon (see Who's Who, p. 219), 10, 24; and the Egyptian Campaign, 68, 69, 72; effect on Egypt, 160

Britain (see also Cromer, Lord and Eden, Sir Antony), landed at Abukir Bay, 72; and Egyptian monuments, 73; interferes in Egypt, 110-12; and Frances support Khedive Ismail, 112; Royal Navy bombards Alexandria, 113-14; Cromer in Egypt, 113-14, 119-23; First World War, 123-4; The Protectorate terminates, 124-5; Anglo-

Egyptian Treaty (1936), 125, 153; and King Faruk in 1942, 148; criticism at home of Lord Killearn, 149; 'Black Saturday' (1952), 154; Anglo-Egyptian Agreement (1954), 158, 169; and France attack Port Said, 158; and the Baghdad Pact, 166, 171, 172; Nasser's unpopularity in, 166, 169, 171; Nasser appeals for arms to, 167; and High Dam, 173-4; and the Suez affair, 175, 176; troops sent to Jordan, 180

British Museum, 78; Rosetta Stone, 72

Browne, W. G., his defence of Muslims, 67; and the hareem system, 86

Bruce, James, 66, 67

Burckhardt, John Lewis (see Who's Who, p. 219), 10, 28; his travels, 75; and the slave trade, 75-6; on the Nubians, 77; his interest in Egyptian antiquities, 77-8

Burton, Sir Richard, 86

CAESAR, Julius, 37-8

Caesareum, the, 38

Caesarion, 38

Cairo (al-Kahira), 121, 20, 21; Nile at, 19; Museum, 26, 29; built, 58; saved from King Amalric, 59; Saracen and other influences on, 60; famine in, 64; architecture of, 66; foreigners in, 66-7; French capitulate in, 72; described by William Hamilton, 73; British Army H.Q. in, 124; Sir Lee Stack murdered in, 125; 1952 riots in, 154; population, 195

Caliphs, Omar, 53, 54, 55; Harun al-Rashid, 57; in tenth century, 58; Fatimid, 58, 59; abolition of the Caliphate, 127-8

Cavafy, C. P., 10

Champollion, Jean-François (see Who's Who, p. 219), and Rosetta Stone inscriptions, 80; mission to Egypt, 81; and the Coptic language, 83

Chateaubriand, Vicomte de, on converts to Islam, 74

Cheops, 27, 28, 29, 30, *6*
Chephren, 29, 30, *1*
Christianity, in Egypt, 39-44; the Crusades, 58-61; and the Muslims, 64, 67
Clement, Bishop of Alexandria, 40-1
Cleopatra, 37-8, *16*
Colvin, Sir Auckland, 111
Constantine, Emperor, 41
Constantinople, 41
Cotton, 67
Cromer, Lord (*see* Who's Who, p. 219), 43; views on Islam, 9, 116; on Ahmed Arabi, 111; Consul-General of Egypt, 113-20; and Mohammed Abdu, 116; on barrier between East and West, 118; and freedom of the Press, 120; leaves Egypt, 120; progress under his administration, 120-1; and Denshawy incident, 121; on government in Egypt, 122-3
Curzon, Hon. Robert, on the English traveller, 8-9; on monks, 83; in Egypt, 83-4; and the hareem system, 86
Cyrus, persecutes the Copts, 44; treats with the Arabs, 53-4

Damascus, 56
Damietta, 7, 60
Dashur, 73
Dayan, General Moshe, 175-6
Deir el-Bahri, temple at, 23, *10*, *11*
Denon, Baron, Dominique-Vivant, 71
Description de l'Egypte, 70, *31*, *32*, *33*, *34*
Din Pasha, Khayr al-, 105-6
Diodorus Siculus, on embalming, 22; Egypt in his *General History*, 37
Dioscorus, 42
Disraeli, Benjamin, and the Suez Canal, 109
Djabarti, Shaikh al- (*see* Who's Who p. 219), on released Mamelukes, 69; admires French learning, 70; opposes Mohammed Ali, 102-3
Drovetti, Bernard, and Egyptian antiquities, 77, 78, 82, *27*
Dufferin, Lord, 113

Duff Gordon, Lady Lucie, *36*; quoted, 7, 9; on the hareem, 87; on social equality, 87-8; on religions, 88; on dancing girls, 88-9; on Europeans in Egypt, 89, 90, 91, 122; on injustices, 90, 91; and Khedive Ismail, 91
Dulles, John Foster (*see* Who's Who, p. 219), 57, against Arab neutralism, 165; fears communism in the Arab world, 167, 174, 177; and High Dam project, 174
Durrell, Lawrence, 10

Eden, Sir Anthony (Lord Avon) (*see* Who's Who, p. 219), 113, *59*; becomes Prime Minister, 166; opposition to Nasser, 171-2, 174
Eisenhower, Dwight David, 175
Elgin, Lord, 72
Emary, Gelil al-, 156
Enfantin, Prosper, 10
Eratosthenes, 36
Euclid, 36

Faisal, King of Iraq, 165, 180
Faruk, King of Egypt (*see* Who's Who, p. 220), 146, 153, 154; and the Italians, 147, 148; and the British Ambassador, 148; and sovereignty over Sudan, 151-2; accused of corruption, 152; rebuffed, 154; deposed, 155
Fawzi, Mahmoud, 156
Forster, E. M., 10; on Cleopatra and Alexandria, 38
Fort Keit Bay, 36
France (*see also* Bonaparte), 197; and Britain in Egypt, 112, 113; and Britain attack Port Said (October 1956), 158; Nasser's unpopularity in, 169; and the Suez affair, 175, 176; and Israel, 175-6
Francis of Assisi, St., 61
Free Officers, the, Neguib elected President of, 154; ruthlessness of, 156
Fuad I, Ahmed, King of Egypt (*see* Who's Who, p. 220), 125
Fustat, al-, Persian's description of, 58-9; burned, 59; in thirteenth century, 60-1

GALLAND, Antoine, publishes *The Thousand and One Nights*, 85
Gardiner, Sir Alan, 82; on Egyptian tradition, 14
Gebel Awlia, dam at, 18
Gibb, H. A. R., Professor, on Islam, 9, 116; and the Romantic influence on Muslim writers, 134-5
Gibbon, Edward, on Christianity in Egypt, 41-2; on anchorites, 43; on persecution in Egypt, 44
Giza, 26-31, 71, 73, 4
Gladstone, William Ewart, and Egypt, 111-12
Glubb Pasha, 171
Gorst, Sir Eldon, 123
Gourna, excavations at, 79
Granville, Lord, 112, 113

HADRIAN, Emperor, 40
Hakim, Tawfik al-, 8, 31-2; and the 1919 Revolution, 126, 159
Halim Pasha, Prince, 109
Hamilton, William, 72-4, 77
Haykal, Mohammed Husayn (*see* Who's Who, p. 220), *Life of Mohammed*, 133-4; *In the Birthplace of Revolution*, 135; quoted, 206-7
Heliopolis, Battle of, 53
Heraclius, Emperor, 44, 54
Hermapolis, monastery at, 43
Herodotus (*see* Who's Who, p. 220), on Egypt, 7, 12; in Egypt, 8; Egyptologists' opinion of, 13; on the Egyptians, 14, 16-17, 20-1; his sources, 14-15; his ideas on the Nile, 16, 17, 18; on embalming, 21-2; compares Greek and Egyptian gods, 23, 24; and Menes, 24-5; and the Pyramids, 26, 27-30; and cleanliness of the Egyptians, 43
Hetepheres, Queen, 29
Hierakonopolis, Temple of, 26
High Dam, the, 18, 196, 198, 70, 71; floods Nubia, 77; financial backing for, 173-4; and ancient monuments preserved by UNESCO, 196-7
Hudeiby, Hasan al-, 157, 158

Husayn, King of Jordan, 171, 172, 180
Husayn, Taha (*see* Who's Who, p. 220), 52; *On Pre-Islamic Poetry*, 128-30; early history of, 129; tried for his views, 129; dismissed from the University, 130; his ideas, 130, 131; and reason and faith, 132-3; and Haykal's influence, 136; quoted, 205

ILLAH, Prince Abd al-, 165; intrigues for Syrian throne, 168; assassinated, 180
Iman, Ibrahim, 155
Irrigation, the Nile dams, 18; in ancient times, 19; canals, 20; and unity of the two Egypts, 25
Islam, 103; English prejudice against, 9; misunderstood, 65; unifies the Ottoman Empire, 70; a divine and civil law, 104; Western attitude toward, 116; and the 1923 Constitution, 127; Haykal defends, 135
Ismail, Khedive, the, 37; and financial affairs, 89, 90, 106-7; and Lady Duff Gordon, 91; absolute ruler, 106; his reforms, 108; and the Suez Canal, 109; deposed, 109
Israel, 64; the Balfour Declaration, 123; Arabs infiltrate into, 167; and the Suez incident, 175-6

JAWHAR, invades Egypt, 58
Jerusalem, and the Crusades, 59

KAMIL, Mustapha (*see* Who's Who, p. 220) and Egyptian nationalism, 118, 119-20; and Aqaba incident, 119; Nasser reads, 145
Karnak, 10, 9
Kassim, Abdul Karim al-, 180, 200
Khartum, Nile at, 18
Kinglake, William, on Islam, 9; on Osman the Scotsman, 75; on Cairo, 89
Kitchener, Lord (*see* Who's Who, p. 220), 44; stops French at Fashoda, 120; British Agent and Consul-General in Egypt, 123

Koran, the, 55, 56; translated by Savary, 67; quoted, 108; in schools, 115; Muslim Brothers and, 150

LAMPSON, Sir Miles (Lord Killearn), and Faruk, 149
Lane, Edward (see Who's Who, p. 220), translates The Thousand and One Nights, 84, 30; on Egyptian freedom in conversation, 85
Lear, Edward, 4
Lepsius, Richard, 82
Lloyd, Lord, High Commissioner for Egypt, 125
Louis IX, King of France, leads 9th Crusade, 61

MADDEN, Dr, on Gourna troglodyte, 79; on Egyptian gods and Christian figures, 84; on Arabs, 89
Maghrabi, Ibn Sa'id al, on al-Fustat, 60-1
Maher Pasha, Aly, 148; and proposed coup d'état, 151
Mamelukes, the, 8, 61; become Sultans of Egypt, 61-2; Bonaparte and, 69; Egyptian attitude to, 70; massacre of, 74; and the French, 101
Manetho, 13, 25
Mankabad, 146, 147
Mansurah, Crusaders defeated at, 61
Mark, Saint, in Alexandria, 39-40
Mecca, pilgrims in, 55; Muslim thought in, 58
Medina, pilgrims in, 55
Mehalla el Kubra, 197, 69
Memphis, history and situation, 25; Alexander visits, 35; pyramids at, 73
Menes, 24-5, 26
Misr-el-Fatat (extremist group led by Ahmed Husayn), 149
Mohammed Ali (see Who's Who, p. 220), 80, 109, 35; becomes ruler of Egypt, 74; permits excavation of ancient tombs, 78; Drovetti reports on, 81; progress under, 90; and reform, 102-4; and al-Tahtawi, 104, 105; revolt against, 107

Mohammed, The Prophet, 53, 115; and government, 104, 127; Taya Husayn's book on, 132; Haykal's Life, 133-4
Mouseion, the, 36, 38
Muhieddin, Zakariya (see Who's Who, p. 221), 199; and the population problem, 195; his efforts to curb inflation, 206
Muslim Brothers, the, history of, 149-51; in Palestine, 152; assassinate Nokrashi, 153; declare jihad against British, 153; support Neguib, 157; and attempted assassination of Nasser, 158; oppose secularization, 160; still influential, 201, 205
Muslims, the, and Europe, 63; W. G. Browne and, 67; Bonaparte and, 69; and the French, 70; integration of converts, 74
Mycerinus, 30, 8
Mythology, 23, 24; Hapi, 19; Osiris and other gods, 24; gods and the Pharaohs, 26; Serapis, 36, 40

NAHAS, Mustapha, 55; exiled, 124; and the British, 148, 149, 153; Prime Minister, 153
Narmer, 26; palette of, 26, 14
Nasser, Gamal Abdel, President (see Who's Who, p. 221), 53, 58, 59, 64; relates Egyptian history to the present, 8; quoted, 10, 101; and the 'Arab circle', 33; and the High Dam, 77, 173-4, 197; and imperialism, 107; and Ahmed Arabi, 110; Eden and, 113, 171-2, 174, 175, background and youth, 145-7; and Young Officers, 148; in battle, 152; thoughts on assassination, 153-4; his genius for intrigue, 154, 158; police and, 154, 155; on pre-Revolutionary vested interests, 155-6; on revolution, 156; the éminence grise, 156-7; and Muslim Brothers, 157, 161; attempted assassination of, 158; disillusioned, 159-60; and secularization, 160-1; and social reform, 162, 189-90, 194-5; and the Arab world, 162, 178-9; and Arab unity,

163, 164, 180, 207, 208; and Nuri
Pasha, 166; attends Bandung Conference, 166; and Britain, 167, 169–70,
171, 202; purchases arms from Czechoslovakia, 167; anti-communist, 168;
exploits Cairo Radio, 171; *The Philosophy of Revolution*, 172; and Suez Canal
incident, 174–5, 176; and Syria, 178–9;
his policy of nationalization, 189–90;
the National Charter, 191–3; delegates
some of his power, 198; and home and
Arab affairs, 200; and the Yemen, 200,
201; and Arab socialism, 204; his
achievements, 205; his problems, 206
Nerval, Gérard de, 10, 87, 89
Neguib, General Mohammed (*see* Who's
Who, p. 221), 53, 56; and humiliation
of Egypt, 149; in battle, 152; President of
Committee of Officers' Club, 154; and
the 1952 Revolution, 155; his popu-
larity, 157; supported by Muslim
Brothers, 157; resigns, 158
Nehru, Jawaharlal, Pandit, 175
Nicaea, Council of, 41
Nile, River, course of, 7, 25, 58; in
ancient Egypt, 12, 13; Delta of, 13, 16,
17–19; flooding of, 14, 19, 73; Hero-
dotus on, 16; Blue and White Nile, 15,
18–19; gauges of, 18, 73; dams, 18, 173;
Osiris and, 24–5; unity of the two
Egypts and, 26; travellers on, 35, 38, 40;
Amr's description of, 56; Volney on, 68
Nilometres, 18
Nokrashi Pasha, and Sudan, 152; and
Israel, 152, 153; assassinated, 153
Nubia, flooded, 77; cartouches in, 80

Octavian, *see* Augustus
Origen, 40, 41
Osman, 74–5
Osman, Sir Amin, assassinated, 151

Palermo Stone, the, 25
Palestine, Zionists and, 151; partition,
152
Palmerston, Lord, and Mohammed Ali,
102

Papyrus, the Turin, 14, 25
Pelusium, 53
Pepi I, 25
Petrie, Sir Flinders, on building the
Pyramids, 28; on the Pharaohs, 30
Pharaohs, the, uncertainty about their
history, 14; religion and, 24; and the
Pyramids, 27–30; position of, 29–30;
Alexander proclaimed, 36; emulated by
Ptolomies, 36
Pharos, the, 36
Plato, on Egyptian tradition, 14; his
influence on Christianity, 40
Pliny (the Younger), on origin of the
Egyptians, 16
Pompey, (the Great), 37
Port Said, Anglo-French attack on, 158
Ptahhotep, Vizier, 30
Ptolemies, the, Ptolemy I Soter, 36;
Egypt under their rule, 36–7; Ptolemy
X, 37; Ptolemy XIV, 37, 38; Ptolemy
XV, 38; end of their rule, 39; and
racial issue, 42; Ptolemy V, 72
Punt (Somaliland), expedition to Land
of, 23, *11*
Pyramids, *4*, *see* individual sites

Ramesses II, 14, *3*
Rawlinson, Sir Henry, and Cuneiform,
80
Raziq, Ali Abd al-, *Islam*, 127–8
Reisner, Dr, 29
Revolution of 1919, breaks out, 123;
explanations for, 126
Rhakotis, *35*, 36
Richard I, King of England, 59
Roberts, David, *21*, *35*
Rommel, Erwin, Field-Marshal, sends
agents to Egypt, 147; in Egypt, 148
Rosellini, Ippolito, and the mission to
Egypt, 81
Rosetta, 7; the Stone, 71–2

Sadat, Anwar al- (*see* Who's Who, p.
221), and Nasser, 146–7; and the
Germans, 147; and plan for *coup d'état*,
151; and 1952 Revolution, 155; *Story of
Arab Unity*, 179; on revolution, 202

Sa'id Pasha, Nuri al- (see Who's Who, p. 221), 165; alarmed about communism in Iraq, 165; favours Western alliance, 166; and Britain, 170, 172; and plot against Syria, 178; assassinated, 180

Saladin (see Who's Who, p. 221), founds the Ayyubid dynasty, 59; his integrity, 59-60

Salem, Gamal, 155

Salt, Henry, 77-8, 81

Saud, King of Saudi Arabia, 178

Savary, Claude-Étienne, 67-8

Sayyed, Dr Lufti al-, 34, 51; efforts for reform, 117; and Egyptian independence, 118, 119; and Aqaba incident, 118, 119; and Taha Husayn, 129, 130; Nasser reads, 145

Selwyn Lloyd, David, 171

Semna, sculptured records at, 18

Sennar, dam at, 18

Serapeum, the, 43

Shafi, Husain al-, 155

Shawki, Ahmed, 155

Shishakli, President of Syria, 168

Sidky Pasha, 151

Sinai, St Catherine's monastery at, 22

Slave trade, the, 75-6; abolished by Khedive Ismail, 108

Snofru, 29, 30

Sphinx, the, Denon on, 71

Sudan, the, Nile dam in, 18; and Britain, 125; Governor-General murdered, 125; and self-government, 151-2; Faruk proclaimed King of, 153; Anglo-Egyptian agreement over, 157

Suez Canal, 198; opening of, 109, 42; the 1956 incident, 11, 158, 60, 61; Amr suggests cutting, 55; building of, 90; Khedive Ismail and, 109; Baring and, 114; threatened by Turkey, 119, 123; British troops on, 124, 153; evacuation of British troops from, 151; Nasser nationalizes, 174

Sulayman, Sidqi, 206

TAHTAWI, Rifa'ah Rafi al-, impact of Europe on his thinking, 104-6

Talleyrand, 69

Tawfik, Khedive, 109; and Ahmed Arabi, 110, 111; British and French support, 112; betrays his cause, 113

Tell el- Kebir, battle of, 113, 38

Thebes, Egyptian antiquities at, 77, 78

Tulun, Ahmed ibn, Governor of Egypt, 57; mosque built by, 57, 23

Tura, the quarries of, 28

Tutankhamen, 32, 13

UNESCO, and the High Dam, 196-7

United Nations, and partition in Palestine, 152; and Israeli army attacks against Egypt, 166; and the Suez affair, 175

United States of America (see also Dulles, J. F.), Nasser's unpopularity in, 169; and the High Dam, 173-4; and communist influence in Egypt, 174; and Syria, 178; send marines to Lebanon, 180

VICTORIA Nyanza, Lake, the Nile and, 18, 19

Volney, Count, C.-F., 68, 69

WADI Halfa, 7, 75

Wadi Natrun, monasteries at, 83, 84

Wafd, the, Mustapha Nahas Pasha becomes leader, 125; and Britain, 125, 148, 153; conflict with the King, 131; Nasser and, 145; wins election, 149; and Muslim Brothers, 153

Wilkinson, Sir Gardiner, 13, 81-2

Wolseley, Sir Garnet, commands British troops, 113

World Bank, and the High Dam, 173, 174

XENOPHANES, 24

YOUNG Officers Revolutionary Committee, the, society founded 1939, 147; infiltrate into the Army, 147; and the Nazis, 149; and Muslim Brothers, 150-1; against Faruk, 155

Young, Thomas, 80

ZAGHLUL, Ahmad Fathi, his translations into Arabic, 117, 118
Zaghlul, Saad (see Who's Who, p. 222), 119, 131, 50; on the heritage from ancient Egypt, 31; Tawfik al-Hakim and, 32; disciple of al-Afghani, 108; Minister of Education, 116; and Cromer, 118; and Aqaba incident, 118; and the 1918 Peace Conference, 124; twice exiled, 124; Prime Minister, 125

Zionists, join British Army, 151